the
better
world
SHOPPING
GUIDE

EVERY DOLLAR MAKES A DIFFERENCE

the
better
world
SHOPPING
GUIDE

Ellis Jones

new society
PUBLISHERS

Cover concept by Ellis Jones. Design by Diane McIntosh.
Images: Getty Images/Photodisc Green.

Printed in Canada.

Inquiries regarding requests to reprint all or part of
The Better World Shopping Guide should be addressed to
New Society Publishers at the address below.

To order directly from the publishers, please call
(250) 247-9737, or order online at www.newsociety.com.

Any other inquiries can be directed by mail to
New Society Publishers
P.O. Box 189, Gabriola Island, BC V0R 1X0, Canada

Library and Archives Canada Cataloguing in Publication

Title: The better world shopping guide / Ellis Jones.

Other titles: Every dollar makes a difference | Shopping guide

Names: Jones, Ellis, 1970– author.

Description: 7th edition. | Includes index.

Identifiers: Canadiana (print) 20220133468 | Canadiana (ebook)
20220133476 | ISBN 9780865719460 (softcover) | ISBN
9781550927399 (PDF) | ISBN 9781771423359 (EPUB)

Subjects: LCSH: Shopping — Moral and ethical aspects —
Handbooks, manuals, etc. | LCSH: Social responsibility of
business — Handbooks, manuals, etc. | LCSH: Commercial
products — Evaluation — Handbooks, manuals, etc. | LCSH:
Green products — Evaluation — Handbooks, manuals, etc. |
LCSH: Consumer education — Handbooks, manuals, etc. |
LCSH: Shopping — Handbooks, manuals, etc. | LCSH: Green
products — Handbooks, manuals, etc. | LCSH: Consumer
education. | LCGFT: Handbooks and manuals.

Funded by the   Financé par le
Government   gouvernement
of Canada   du Canada

New Society Publishers' mission is to publish books that contribute
in fundamental ways to building an ecologically sustainable and just
society, and to do so with the least possible impact on the environment, in a manner that models this vision.

MIX
Paper from
responsible sources
FSC® C016245

Contents

APPRECIATION

I am very grateful to Paul Todisco, Collin Ahrens, Ross Haenfler, J.P. Meyer, James Beam, Warren Zeger, Kristin Wallace, Mark Fairbrother, Tom McGlynn, Jason Logan, Brett Jacobs, and Jacob O'Brien for their hard work testing the guide and researching brands in the real world. And to my wife, Ara Francis, for her unwavering advocacy and dedication to getting this project the recognition and support it deserves. Also, a very special thank-you to the good people at Free Range, Christie Communications, and The Pachamama Alliance who have been incredible in making important connections for me around this work. Finally, I want to grant my deepest gratitude to everyone at The Amity Foundation for being amazing alllies for this work while doing such extraordinary work on their own to build a better world for us all.

I am also very grateful to you, the reader, for picking up this book. I'd like to say (because you may never hear it from anyone else) on behalf of all of the people on this planet whom you will never meet and all the natural places you will never see...

Thank you.

7TH EDITION NOTES

A decade and a half after the 1st edition was published, I am humbled to think that this little book has sold around 200,000 copies.

In 2022, even more of us are beginning to understand the fragility of our democracy and its vulnerability to powerful interest groups. Given the global pandemic, climate change, income inequality, racial injustice, and the attempted overthrow of our last deomcratic election, the connections between economics and politics have become difficult to ignore.

This particular edition has taken a few extra years to produce, but hopefully it will have been worth the wait. In this edition you'll find:

✓ More than 2,000 companies evaluated
✓ A simpler, more practical grading system
✓ New charts on Big Tech, Climate Change, etc.
✓ Sample report cards for each grade
✓ More ways to engage beyond this book!

Let's reclaim our democracy
while we still have time.

THE WEBSITE

This guide is far too small to contain the wide range of data used to generate rankings for each company. If you are interested in more specifics on how individual companies are rated, and exactly what is taken into account, you can visit the website. It also contains updated ratings, direct links to resources, and new product categories that have been added since the writing of this guide.

You can also connect with me directly through the website. I'd be happy to give a presentation, lecture, workshop, or even host a live Q&A session in person, over the phone, or online. Whether you're interested in this for your school, college, office, festival, conference, retreat, annual meeting, reunion, or for your whole community, reach out to me. There is plenty of work to be done in this area, and I'd love to share what I've learned with you so that you can pursue your own piece of the better world puzzle more effectively. It will take all of us working together to build a brighter future.

sodoctorjones@gmail.com

www.betterworldshopper.org

THE APP

You should also know that there is now a smart-phone app available for iOS and Android phones. "Better World Shopper" based on the same data as this book. While it does not provide all of the useful information you'll find in this guide, it does give you instant access to all of the rankings. Having this information at your fingertips can turn out to be really useful, particularly when you forget to bring the book with you. And, at the moment, it's free, so there's no reason not to download it.

Take a look at it. Let me know what I should add to it. You can also contact me directly through the app if you want me to give a virtual talk to your group, organization, annual meeting, non-profit, conference, festival, high school, college, university, church, temple, synagogue, book-store, office gathering, or seminar. And, as soon as this pandemic eases up a bit, I'd be thrilled to come visit in person! We can only build this work into what it needs to be by working together.

Let's support each other.

www.betterworldshopper.org

THE OTHER APPS

As it turns out, I've been busy creating a couple of apps that this work has inspired.

First, if you're tired of trying to figure out which news outlets are trustworthy and which aren't, which are skewing liberal or conservative and which are neutral, and which to recommend to friends and family who have fallen down a media rabbit hole, it turns out that this same data-driven system has a few answers. *Media Glass* is an app that rates news sources based on their fact-based integrity as well as their political leanings. It is the perfect place to assess the nutritional value of your own news diet and even improve it. News sources rated from A to F.

Next, if you're having difficulty navigating the fraught landscape of politicians who seem to often talk out of both sides of their mouths, then you should take a look at the honesty report cards in *Voter Glass*. US politicians (left and right) are rated from A to F based solely on publicly available fact-checking data. Sometimes it's very useful to know who is lying to you. This app should help with that piece of the puzzle.

www.betterworldshopper.org

SOCIAL MEDIA

This is still early days for my social media adventures, but I am beginning to move into the 21st century. You can find my new YouTube channel, *Better World Toolkit*, with a handful of assorted videos that go beyond just shopping and delve into deeper questions regarding corporate responsibility, political corruption, and media integrity. Submit your own questions in the comments to motivate me to post new videos in order to answer them. I've started to actually enjoy the process.

You can also reach out to me through a variety of my other social media accounts, although I may not always respond as quickly as post.

YouTube: *Better World Toolkit*

Facebook: Ellis Jones
LinkedIn: Dr. Ellis Jones
Twitter: @sodoctorjones
Venmo: @sodoctorjones
Skype: sodoctorjones
Instagram: sodoctorjones

Email: sodoctorjones@gmail.com

THE DOCUMENTARY

In 2021, the wonderful folks at The Amity Foundation, with the help of the filmmaker, Thijs Boonen, premiered a short documentary (30 min) of my research, *Every Dollar Is A Vote*, at the Colorado Environmental Film Festival. I am honored to have been the subject of such a lovingly crafted representation of the work that I've been doing for the past two decades. While, it is by no means comprehensive, it should give you a feeling for the connections that I've been attempting to make between how we spend our dollars and the future of our democracy, our economy, our fellow human beings, and our survival potential on this planet for the foreseeable future. I'm not certain how I feel about seeing myself on a big screen. To be honest, it's a bit awkward, but the work is important enough that I will get over myself. You be the judge of its usefulness.

If you're interested in watching it, reach out and I'll find some way to get you access to the latest version of it to screen at your next gathering with friends or colleagues. Watch the trailer on YouTube by searching for the *Better World Toolkit* channel.

sodoctorjones@gmail.com

THE PROBLEM

Money is power. Perhaps more than any generation that has come before us, we understand the deeply rooted reality of this short phrase and its universal meaning for every human being living on this planet.

It follows that wherever large amounts of money collect, so also new centers of power form. The latest historical manifestation of this is the modern corporation. As trillions of dollars accumulate in the corporate sphere, we witness the growing power of corporations to shape the world as they see fit.

This power is not limited to controlling the face of our own government through consistent, record-breaking campaign contributions, but also the fate of millions of people and the planet itself through jobs, resource exploitation, pollution, working conditions, energy consumption, forest destruction, and so on.

Make no mistake, these new power centers are not democracies. We don't vote for the CEOs or their policies (unless we are rich enough to be significant shareholders who are informed enough to know what's going on and compassionate enough to care about more than just personal profit), yet our destinies are increasingly in their hands.

THE SOLUTION

As these power centers shift, we must shift our own voices if we wish to be heard. As citizens, on average, we might vote once every four years, if at all. As consumers, we vote every single day with the purest form of power…money. The average American family spends around $25,000 every year on goods and services. Think of it as casting 25,000 votes every year for the kind of world you want to live in.

Unfortunately, as difficult as it is to find good, solid information on candidates during an election year, it's often even harder to find good, solid information on corporations. Our current laws are so lax that half of the time we can't even figure out which brands belong to which companies (they don't have to tell us), much less have any idea of what their business practices look like.

For the past two decades, I've dedicated myself to researching this very problem by compiling a database of every reliable source of information available on corporate behavior and synthesizing the information into a single report card grade for every company. The result is this book. Use it to reclaim your true vote. Use it to build a better world.

THE ISSUES

➤ HUMAN RIGHTS: child labor, sweatshops, slavery, worker health and safety records, human trafficking, developing-world exploitation, international health issues, economic divestment, union busting, fair trade, worker fatalities, livable wages, democratic principles.

➤ THE ENVIRONMENT: climate change, renewable energy, toxic waste, recycling, eco-innovations, sustainable farming, ocean conservation, rainforest destruction, ecosystem impacts, overall pollution.

➤ ANIMAL PROTECTION: humane treatment, factory farming, animal habitat preservation, sustainable seafood harvesting, animal testing, animal-free alternatives, vegan-friendliness.

➤ COMMUNITY INVOLVEMENT: family farms, non-profit alliances, local businesses, sustainable growth, campaign contributions, paid lobbyists, political corruption, greenwashing, transparency.

➤ SOCIAL JUSTICE: harassment, discrimination (based on race, gender, age, sexuality, ability, religion, ethnicity), class action lawsuits, unethical business practices, government fines, cover-ups, illegal activities, executive pay.

THE SOURCES

Here is a list of a few of the resources used to assess the overall social and environmental responsibility of the companies in this guide:

[AH]   American Humane Association
[AYS]   As You Sow: CEO Salaries & Packaging
[CCC]   Clean Clothes Campaign
[CC]   Climate Counts: Global Warming Score
[CER]   CERES: Climate Change Research
[CRP]   Center for Responsive Politics
[CSP]   Center for Science in the Public Interest
[CW]   Corpwatch: Greenwash Awards
[EC]   Ethical Consumer: Rankings & Boycotts
[EPA]   US Environmental Protection Agency
[FTF]   Fair Trade Federation: FT Certified
[FTW]   Free2Work: Human Trafficking
[GAM]   Green America: Certified Green Business
[GP]   Greenpeace: Sustainable Seafood
[HRC]   Human Rights Campaign: Equality Index
[ILRF] International Labor Rights Forum
[OXF]   Oxfam International
[PERI] Political Economy Research Institute
[SAI]   Social Accountability International
[SEC]   Securites and Exchange Commission
[SVT]   Silicon Valley Toxics Coalition
[UCS]   Union of Concerned Scientists

For a more comprehensive list visit, www.betterworldshopper.org

THE RANKINGS

STEP 1: Over 35 years' worth of data has been collected from a wide range of public, private, and nonprofit sources, tracking information on one or more of the five issue areas that make up the overall responsibility picture for companies that create the products and services we use every day.

STEP 2: The data is organized into a massive database of more than 2,000 companies that matches each individual company with its brands; assigns appropriate weights to each piece of data based on its quality, reliability, and scope; and calculates an overall social and environmental responsibility score for each company from −100 to +100.

STEP 3: Companies and brands are transferred to smaller, more specific data charts based on common product categories, where each is assigned a letter grade based on its overall responsibility. This highly organized grading system allows consumers to maximize the impact of their dollars regardless of what they're purchasing.

THE RANKINGS

STEP 4: Researchers are sent to supermarkets, natural foods stores, and retail outlets across the country to identify those products that are most commonly available to the average consumer to make sure that what you see on the shelves matches what you see in the book. Those particular companies and brands are then transferred into the easy-to-use report cards that make up the bulk of the shopping guide.

STEP 5: As regular data sources release their latest findings, they are added to the database. Also, as new third-party sources of data are identified, they are evaluated for potential inclusion in the ranking system. Mergers and buyouts are tracked so that their effects on the rankings can be noted. Updated rankings are regularly made available online through the website until a new edition of the shopping guide can be published.

As readers, your comments and suggestions are invaluable. Please contact me if you have ideas on how to improve the rating system.

FREQUENTLY ASKED QUESTIONS

"Isn't it more important to buy less rather than worry about the kind of stuff we're buying?"

Both are equally important. As we've learned from the voluntary simplicity movement, we must reduce our quantity of consumption if we are to have any reasonable future. At the same time, we must increase the quality of our consumption so that every dollar spent helps build a better tomorrow rather than bring about its destruction. While I wholeheartedly support the former, this book deals mainly with the latter.

"What if I don't have access to or can't afford many of the products that receive 'A' ratings?"

Don't give up! It's important to choose the best option available to you depending on your location and resources, both of which will likely change many times in your life. Sometimes the choice is between a 'C' brand and an 'F' brand, and that is just as important a choice to make. I, myself, strive to maintain an overall shopping GPA of 'B+' — and even then, I'm not always successful. Remember, as with voting, there is always a choice to be made, imperfect as it may be.

FREQUENTLY ASKED QUESTIONS

"Isn't this 'buying green' just something to make us feel better rather than something that will actually lead to real change?"

No. Trillions of dollars circulate in the global economy, driven primarily by consumers. These are our dollars that are shaping the fate of this world, and we must begin taking responsibility for their collective impact. Dollars (like votes) add up very quickly and can lead to powerful changes in both the short and long term.

"Shouldn't we be voting, demonstrating, and organizing within our political system?"

Yes. We need to bring transparency, accountability, and responsibility to both our political AND economic systems. If we address only one, our efforts will ultimately fail. So, do not use this guide as an excuse to shift focus away from our political problems — the two go hand in hand.

"How do I find out more details about a particular company or the ranking system as a whole?"

Email me, or better yet, invite me out to come talk about it!

WHAT DO THE GRADES MEAN?

✪	**Top 1% of all companies.**
A	Social and environmental leaders in their respective industries.
B	Noteworthy progress improving their social and environmental impacts.
C	Mixed records of overall responsibility and/or insufficient data available.
D	Significantly negative social and environmental impacts noted.
F	Some of the worst companies based on overall social and environmental data.
X	**Bottom 1% of all companies.**

STAR COMPANY PROFILE

NEW RESOURCE BANK

☆ Green America Certified Green Business[40]
☆ San Francisco Certified Green Business[27]
☆ Social Venture Network member[66]
☆ Certified Benefit Corporation (B Corp)[70]
☆ 100% Wind Power, EPA Certified[27]
☆ LEED Gold Certified headquarters[3]
☆ Member, American Sustainable Business Council[48]
☆ Car-sharing program offered to all employees for meetings[40]
☆ Offers a debit card that donates to environmental orgs with each purchase

OVERALL GRADE: ✪

[TOP 1%]

For more details, you can look up the source reference number in the DATA SOURCES section.

'A' COMPANY
PROFILE

CLIF BAR

☆ Green Cross Environmental Leader Award[41]
☆ EPA — Green Power Award Winner, 3 years[70]
☆ GAM certified Green Business[40]
☆ 100% Green Power Purchaser[70]
☆ Affiliate, Social Accountability International[65]
☆ Member, 1% For The Planet[1]
☆ Member, Social Venture Network[66]
☆ Member, Ceres Coalition Companies[15]
☆ Rated 72/100 for Climate Commitment[19]
☆ Business Ethics Award Winner[8]

○ Mid-level organic label integrity[21]

OVERALL GRADE: A

[TOP 15%]

For more details, you can look up the source
reference numbers in the DATA SOURCES section.

'B' COMPANY PROFILE

STAPLES

☆ EPA — 100% Green Power Purchaser[70]
☆ Green Power Award Winner, 6 years[70]
☆ LGBTQ Equality Index Score of 93/100[46]
☆ 'B' for the social & environmental impacts of their paper supply process[36]

○ CERES — Climate Change Score 43/100[15]
○ Former target of AFL-CIO boycott[73]

☠ $1 million in campaign contributions[12]
☠ $2 million paid to political lobbyists[12]

OVERALL GRADE: B

[TOP 33%]

For more details, you can look up the source
reference number in the DATA SOURCES section.

'C' COMPANY PROFILE

GENERAL MILLS

☆ EPA — 100% Green Power Purchaser[70]
☆ Member, Fair Trade USA[34]
☆ Affiliate, Social Accountability International[65]
☆ LGBTQ Equality Index Score of 100/100[46]

○ Rated 'C' for overall social responsibility[61]
○ Rated 62/100 for Climate Commitment[19]
○ 'B-' for marketing junk food to children[13]

☠ Rated 40/100 social/environmental impacts[56]
☠ Rated 'D' for plastic packaging pollution[4]
☠ Rated 22/100 for Climate Responsibility[15]
☠ Low ratings for organic label integrity[21]

OVERALL GRADE: C

[MIDDLE 33%]

For more details, you can look up the source
reference numbers in the DATA SOURCES section.

'D' COMPANY PROFILE

SONY

☆ Rated 82/100 Sourcing of Conflict Minerals[70]
☆ LGBTQ Equality Index Score of 90/100[46]
☆ Rated 85/100 for Climate Commitment[19]

○ Rated 'C' for labor in electronics industry[15]
○ Rated 'C' for use of intl forced labor[73]

☠ Rated 'F' for overall social responsibility[61]
☠ $10 million in campaign contributions[12]
☠ $54 million paid to political lobbyists[12]
☠ Former member of ALEC, a shadowy pro-corporate, Washington lobbying group[78]
☠ 'F' for marketing junk food to children[13]
☠ Rated 'D+' for eco-responsibility in industry[44]

OVERALL GRADE: D

[BOTTOM 33%]

For more details, you can look up the source
reference numbers in the DATA SOURCES section.

'F' COMPANY PROFILE

FACEBOOK

- ☠ 33/100 on climate change actions taken[19]
- ☠ $5.8 million in fines paid for legal violations of privacy, discrimination, campaign finance[77]
- ☠ $17 million in campaign contributions[12]
- ☠ $115 million paid to political lobbyists[12]
- ☠ #53 in Top 100 List of Most Overpaid CEOs[4]
- ☠ Former member of ALEC, a shadowy pro-cor-porate, Washington lobbying group[78]
- ☠ 'D' for clean energy transparency[44]
- ☠ Named "monopoly" by FTC for long-term anti-competitive practices in social media[79]
- ☠ Internal memos reveal company knows that it is harming children and democracy[80]
- ☠ US Justice Dept suit — worker discrimina-tion[81]

OVERALL GRADE: F

[BOTTOM 15%]

For more details, you can look up the source reference numbers in the DATA SOURCES section.

'X' COMPANY PROFILE

KOCH INDUSTRIES

- ☠ #14 of Toxic 100 Water Polluters[58]
- ☠ #23 of Toxic 100 Greenhouse Gas Polluters[58]
- ☠ #24 of Toxic 100 Air Polluters[58]
- ☠ Founding member of shadowy American Legislative Exchange Council (ALEC)[78]
- ☠ US Justice Dept imposes largest fines in history for over 300 oil spills[81]
- ☠ $67 million in campaign contributions[12]
- ☠ $166 million paid to political lobbyists[12]
- ☠ $929 million in fines paid for violations of environmental, workplace safety, health, price-fixing, and consumer-protection laws[77]
- ☠ One of 12 major companies blocking climate change legislation[44]

OVERALL GRADE: X

[BOTTOM 1%]

For more details, you can look up the source
reference numbers in the DATA SOURCES section.

THE 20 BEST LIST

1. GUAYAKI
2. ALTER ECO
3. SEVENTH GENERATION
4. PATAGONIA
5. NEW BELGIUM BREWING
6. ORGANIC VALLEY
7. NEW LEAF PAPER
8. METHOD
9. AMALGAMATED BANK
10. EQUAL EXCHANGE
11. NUMI TEA
12. DR. BRONNER'S
13. BETTER WORLD CLUB
14. GROUNDS FOR CHANGE
15. PRESERVE
16. NUTIVA
17. ECOVER
18. KLEAN KANTEEN
19. EO BODY CARE
20. NATURE'S PATH

Rankings are based on overall social and environmental records.

THE 20 WORST LIST

1. EXXON-MOBIL
2. KRAFT
3. WALMART
4. CHEVRON-TEXACO
5. GENERAL ELECTRIC
6. GENERAL MOTORS
7. PFIZER
8. DOW CHEMICAL
9. KOCH INDUSTRIES
10. CITIBANK
11. NESTLÉ
12. BP
13. AT&T
14. SHELL
15. BOEING
16. CONOCOPHILLIPS
17. VERIZON
18. ABBOTT LABORATORIES
19. DUKE ENERGY
20. MONSANTO

Rankings are based on overall social and environmental records.

THE TOP 10 CLIMATE ACTIONS

1. REDUCE ALL GAS/OIL USE
2. PLANT-BASED DIET
3. CONSERVE ELECTRICITY
4. VOTE EVERY YEAR
5. FLY LESS OFTEN
6. JOIN AN ECO-ORGANIZATION
7. INSTALL SOLAR PANELS
8. ELIMINATE PLASTICS
9. WEATHERIZE YOUR HOME
10. PRESSURE GOVT OFFICIALS

The above list includes 10 of the most effective ways you can help combat climate change. We'll ultimately need deep, systemic changes to be successful, but you can also become part of the solution right now while we all push for more substantive social change.

THE TOP 10 THINGS TO CHANGE

1. BANKS
2. GASOLINE
3. SUPERMARKETS
4. RETAIL STORES
5. CARS
6. SEAFOOD
7. CHOCOLATE
8. COFFEE / TEA
9. CREDIT CARDS
10. CLEANING PRODUCTS

If you want to begin with the changes that will make the most difference for people and the planet, start with these 10 things. They are listed in order of importance based on my own research into these industries.

THE 10 BIGGEST SUCCESS STORIES

	GRADE CHANGE	'06 ▸ '22
1.	EO BODY CARE	B⁺ ▸ ★
2.	GREEN FOREST	B ▸ A
3.	SAN-J	C ▸ A
4.	DANNON	C ▸ B
5.	GAP CLOTHING	C⁺ ▸ B
6.	SOUTHWEST AIR	D⁺ ▸ B
7.	METHOD	** ▸ ★
8.	PANGEA ORGANICS	** ▸ A
9.	ECO LIPS	** ▸ ★
10.	CHIPOTLE	** ▸ A

The above list includes the six companies that, as of early 2022, have shown the most improvement since the first edition of the book was released, as well as four companies that weren't listed in the original edition (noted by **). Every one of these companies is a demonstration of what a deep commitment to a better world can achieve given enough time and effort.

THE 10 BIGGEST DISAPPOINTMENTS

GRADE CHANGE	'06 ▶ '22
1. BURT'S BEES	A⁻ ▶ C
2. BP	A⁻ ▶ X
3. PEPSI	B ▶ D
4. FEDEX	B ▶ D
5. CADBURY	B⁻ ▶ D
6. GERBER	C⁺ ▶ X
7. KELLOGG'S	C⁺ ▶ D
8. UNILEVER	C ▶ D
9. PROCTER & GAMBLE	C ▶ F
10. BANK OF AMERICA	C⁻ ▶ F

The above list includes the 10 companies that, as of early 2022, have fallen from the top of their respective industries to the middle, or worse, from the middle to the very bottom. It is essential that we, as consumers, send a clear message that we will no longer reward companies for this kind of irresponsible behavior.

THE TOP 10 BAILOUT LIST

1.	AIG	70
2.	CITIBANK	50
3.	BANK OF AMERICA	45
4.	GENERAL MOTORS	31
5.	J.P. MORGAN	25
6.	WELLS FARGO	25
7.	CHRYSLER	12
8.	MORGAN STANLEY	10
9.	GOLDMAN SACHS	10
10.	PNC FINANCIAL	8

We are quickly learning that unless we, as consumers, can keep companies responsible in the marketplace, we may end up paying for their irresponsible behavior with our own taxpayer dollars.

The above list includes the 10 companies that, by mid-2009, had received the most bailout money from the US taxpayers. The figures on the right represent how much we have spent, in billions, bailing these companies out.[54]

THE TOP 10 LOBBYIST LIST

1. BLUE CROSS/SHIELD   416
2. AT&T   395
3. GENERAL ELECTRIC   374
4. KRAFT   331
5. VERIZON   295
6. EXXON MOBIL   289
7. COMCAST   234
8. PFIZER   221
9. GENERAL MOTORS   212
10. MICROSOFT   193

It's important to understand that we are not the only ones learning to turn our dollars into votes. These are some of the loudest economic voices in Washington.

The above list includes 10 companies currently spending some of the largest amounts of money on Washington lobbyists to influence the democratic process in ways that serve their own interests. The figures on the right represent how much they have spent, in millions, over the past twenty-four years.[12]

WHO OWNS WHO?

COMPANY	OWNED BY
1. WHOLE FOODS	AMAZON
2. SEVENTH GEN	UNILEVER
3. BURT'S BEES	CLOROX
4. TOM'S OF MAINE	COLGATE
5. STONYFIELD	DANONE
6. BEN & JERRY'S	UNILEVER
7. AVEDA	L'OREAL
8. NEW CHAPTER	P & G
9. HONEST TEA	COCA-COLA
10. ANNIE'S	GEN MILLS

The above list includes the 10 companies that people are most surprised to find out are owned by larger companies that don't always share the values of the former.

Don't assume, however, that these companies are no longer socially and environmentally responible. According to the data, many of them have maintained most or all of their social and environmental responsibility.

INDEPENDENTLY OWNED

1. CLIF
2. DR. BRONNER'S
3. ALTER ECO
4. EQUAL EXCHANGE
5. ORGANIC VALLEY
6. PATAGONIA
7. KLEAN KANTEEN
8. NATURE'S PATH
9. EDEN FOODS
10. CHIPOTLE

The above list includes 10 companies that have yet to be purchased by larger multinational corporations with unknown intentions. While our financial system currently incentivizes purchasing smaller companies as an effective "growth strategy," the results are not always best for consumers or citizens.

These 10 companies could "cash out" at any point, but for now, they are holding on to their independence despite the odds.

THE NEWS

It's become clear that how we consume our daily news may be as important, if not more important, as what we purchase at the supermarket, department store, or online.

I have applied the same data-driven approach that underpins the research for the products and services in these guides for the past 15 years and adapted it to rate news sources based on: reliability, integrity, neutrality, independence, transparency, and fact-based reporting.

I've organized the results into three charts: center, left, and right. Use these charts to help your friends, your family, and yourself find more thoughtful sources of news. Whether you lean left, right, or neutral, there are better and worse sources of news to consume.

Improve your media diet the way you might improve the nutritional value of the food you eat, slowy and methodically, with a lot of forgiveness built in. Try and rely on sources rated 'B' or better. It's OK to dip into 'C' and 'D' sources every now and then, but avoid 'F' and 'X' sources if at all possible. Lists within grade ranges are organized alphabetically.

For more details, you can download Media Glass, the smartphone app for iOS and Android.

NEWS - CENTER

✪	AP, CSPAN, Financial Times, New York Times, NPR, PBS, Politico, Reuters
A	ABC, Al Jazeera, The Atlantic, AXIOS, BBC, Bloomberg, CBS, CDC, Chicago Sun Times, Chicago Tribune, Christian Science Monitor, Consumer Reports, The Conversation, Fact Check, FiveThirtyEight, Gallup, Guardian, IJR, LA Times, National Geographic, NBC, Newsday, Newsy, Daily News, Politifact, PRI, ProPublica, Quartz, Reason, The Skimm, TIME, USA Today, Wall St Journal, Washington Post, Weather Channel, WHO
B	Boston Globe, Boston Herald, CNET, Globe & Mail, Google News, LA Daily News, Miami Herald, Newsweek, OZY, Philadelphia Inquirer, SF Chronicle, Snopes, US News & World, Wikipedia, Yahoo News
C	Buzzfeed, CNN, Forbes, The Observer (UK), Orange County Register, TMZ
D	Daily Mail, Washington Times
F	
X	

NEWS - LEFT

⊛	
A	Al Jazeera, The Atlantic, Chicago Sun Times, Common Dreams, Guardian, Houston Chronicle, The Independent, LA Times, NY Daily News, New Yorker, Newsday, ProPublica, The Root, The Skimm
B	CNET, Daily Beast, Democracy Now, Google News, Huffpost, Miami Herald, Mother Jones, The Nation, New Republic, Newsweek, OZY, The Progressive, Rolling Stone, Salon, SF Chronicle, Slate, The Verge, VICE, Vox, Yahoo News
C	Buzzfeed, CNN, Facebook News, Mashable, MSNBC, MTV News, The Observer (UK), TMZ, Washington Monthly
D	Boing Boing, Care2, Counter Punch, Daily Kos, Raw Story, Think Progress, TYT
F	Democratice National Committee, Free Speech TV, Palmer Report, Wonkette
X	**Occupy Democrats**

NEWS - RIGHT

★	
A	Christianity Today, Detroit News, Fiscal Times, Fortune, Independent Journal Review (IJR), Market Watch, Rasmussen Reports, Reason, Wall Street Journal
B	Boston Herald, The Bulwark, Dallas Morning News, The Dispatch, Globe & Mail, LA Daily News, National Interest, New York Observer, Weekly Standard
C	American Conservative, Commentary, Independent Institute, Intellectual Conservative, Libertarian Republic, Orange County Register, Real Clear Politics
D	Daily Mail, Daily Telegraph, National Review, New York Post, Newsmax, Sinclair, The Washington Times
F	The Blaze, Breitbart, OAN, FOX News, Red State, Republican National Committee
X	Conservative Tribune, Gateway Pundit, Info Wars, News Punch, QAnon, WND

WHAT IF I CAN'T FIND A COMPANY?

While this guide is meant to be comprehensive, it is far from complete. You will likely encounter companies and brands on the shelves that don't show up in these pages. Here are a few simple guidelines that should help you:

If an unknown company's products are certified fair trade, you may assume that it falls into the A- range.

If an unknown company's products are certified organic, you may assume that it falls into the B+ range.

If you don't know anything at all about a particular company or brand, assume that it falls into the C range.

Unknown companies producing clothing, electronics, or shoes should be assumed to have a D or F.

If you wish to see a more detailed version of these rankings or ask about a particular company that you can't find in the guide, you're welcome to visit:

www.betterworldshopper.org

HOW TO USE THIS SHOPPING GUIDE

This book is meant to be used as a practical guide while shopping at the supermarket, in the mall, or online. Familiarize yourself with the alphabetical listing of categories and dog-ear any pages you find particularly useful.

Utilize the rankings on the left as a quick guide to any product you're thinking about buying. Note that all rankings are relative to their product category, so a company may shift up or down depending on its competition.

Useful information and helpful tips appear on the right along with a quick sketch of some of the differences between the best and worst companies. At the bottom of the page are links to online resources to learn more about some of the companies listed.

The book has been purposefully made small so that you can keep it with you in your purse, backpack, briefcase, or pocket. Find a convenient place for it now, while you're reading this sentence. Whatever you do, don't put it on a shelf!

www.betterworldshopper.org

AIRLINES

✪	
A	
B	Alaska, Southwest, JetBlue, Virgin, Delta
C	KLM, Air France, Easy Jet, Lufthansa, British Airways, Singapore, Cathay Pacific, Qantas, JAL, ANA, Allegiant, Korean Air, SAS, AirTran, Aer Lingus, Air Canada, Express Jet, Sky West, Air New Zealand
D	Frontier, Spirit
F	American Airlines, United
X	

AIRLINES

2022 RANKINGS

1. Alaska
2. Southwest
3. JetBlue
4. Virgin
5. Delta
6. Allegiant
7. Frontier
8. Spirit
9. American
10. United

BETTER CHOICE

JetBlue

☆ Perfect 100 on HRC Equality Index
☆ Industry leader in treatment of passengers
☆ Offers carbon offsets & green food options

WORST CHOICE

United

☠ RS 'F' for recycling efforts in the industry[61]
☠ Paid $90 million to Washington lobbyists[12]
☠ Named global climate change laggard[15]

USEFUL RESOURCES
🖥 sustainabletravel.org

APPLIANCES & HARDWARE

★	Preserve, Recycline
A	TerraCycle, Old Fashioned Milk Paint
B	Ace Hardware, WD-40, Norelco, Cuisinart, EGO
C	Siemens, Electrolux, Frigidaire, Dyson, JCB, DeLonghi, Dewalt, Wahl, Haier, Krups, BSH, Sunbeam, Dremel, RYOBI, Miele, Remington, Sherwin Williams, Acme, Dutch Boy, Stanley, Black & Decker, Hoover, Magic Chef, Sylvania, Bosch
D	Sanyo, Whirlpool, Maytag, KitchenAid, 3M, Admiral, Braun, T-fal, Daewoo, Hitachi, Owens Corning, Philips, Samsung, SONY, LG, Panasonic, Home Depot, Lowe's, Emerson, Sears, Kenmore, Kmart
F	Costco
X	GE, Walmart

APPLIANCES & HARDWARE

WHAT YOU NEED TO KNOW

Whether it's major home improvement efforts or just small kitchen appliances, the hardware you buy for your house has a significant impact on the people abroad who help manufacture it.

BUYING TIPS

✓ Look for products with Energy Star labels

WORST CHOICE

Walmart

☠ MM's "Worst Corporation" list for three years[51]

☠ Major toxic waste dumping fines[25]

☠ CEP 'F' for overall social responsibility[14]

☠ Documented exploitation of child labor[61]

WORST CHOICE

GE (General Electric)

☠ MM's "Worst Corporation" list for five years[51]

☠ #34 in "Top 100 Corporate Criminals"[51]

☠ Target of "War Profiteer" campaign[61]

☠ Paid $374 million to Washington lobbyists[12]

USEFUL RESOURCES

🖥 www.energystar.gov

BABY CARE

⭐	Seventh Generation
A	gDiapers, Plum Organics, Ella's Kitchen, Earth Mama, Happy Baby, Healthy Times, Peapods, Organic Baby, Tender Care, Tushies, Earth's Best, Jason, Weleda
B	TastyBaby, Huggies, GoodNites, Baby Magic, Mr. Bubble
C	Playtex, Nature's Gate, Graco, Boudreaux's, Britax, Chicco, Evenflo, Playmates, Avent, Oshkosh
D	Carter's, Nature's Goodness, Church & Dwight, Arm & Hammer, Del Monte, Enfamil, Q-Tips, Vaseline, Chiquita
F	Johnson & Johnson, Aveeno, Coppertone, Disney, Baby Einstein, Pampers, Luvs
X	Gerber, Nestlé, Nabisco, Pedialyte, Pediasure, Similac

BABY CARE

WHAT YOU NEED TO KNOW

Infants and toddlers are more vulnerable to the effects of harmful chemicals and pesticides, so if you're going to buy anything organic, it should be something from this category.

BEST CHOICE

Seventh Generation

☆ Ranked #2 best company on the planet
☆ Empowers consumers w/packaging
☆ Winner, Sustainability Report Award
☆ Socially Responsible Business Award

BETTER CHOICE

gDiapers

☆ B Lab Certified Responsible Company
☆ GAM certified Green Business
☆ Developed cloth/disposable hybrid diaper

WORST CHOICE

Gerber (Nestlé)

☠ Baby formula human rights boycott[48]
☠ "Most Irresponsible" corporation award[6]
☠ Involved in child slavery lawsuit[61]
☠ Aggressive takeovers of family farms[61]

BAKED GOODS & BAKING SUPPLIES

⭐	Nature's Path
A	King Arthur, Eden, Bob's Red Mill, Ener-G, Rapunzel, Spectrum, Hain, Arrowhead Mills
B	Vernmont Bread, Sun-Maid
C	Hodgson Mill, Pillsbury, Betty Crocker, Quaker, Gold Medal, Bisquick, Ghirardelli, Krusteaz, Dr. Oetker, Mother's, Little Debbie, Hostess,
D	Hershey, Borden, Eagle Brand, Kellogg's, Keebler, Arm & Hammer, Contadina, Cake Mate, Diamond
F	Banquet, Conagra, Duncan Hines
X	Nestlé, Carnation, Nabisco, Albers, Kraft, Jell-O, Planters, Libby's

BAKED GOODS & BAKING SUPPLIES

BUYING TIPS
✓ Buy organic baking products when available

BEST CHOICE
Nature's Path

☆ GAM certified Green Business
☆ Named one of Canada's Greenest Employers
☆ Sponsors environmental efforts and festivals

BETTER CHOICE
King Arthur Flour

☆ 100% employee-owned company
☆ Awarded "Most Democratic Workplace"
☆ Business Ethics award winner
☆ B Lab Certified Responsible Company
☆ BBB's Torch Award for ethics

WORST CHOICE
Jell-O (Kraft)

☠ MM's "Worst Corporation" list for five years[51]
☠ Currently target of two major boycotts[22,55]
☠ Greenwash Award for public deception[25]
☠ Named global climate change laggard[15]
☠ Paid $331 million to Washington lobbyists[12]

BANKS & CREDIT CARDS

✪	**New Resource Bank, Amalgamated Bank**
A	Sunrise Banks, Beneficial State, Vancity, Alternatives CU, Hope Federal CU, Self Help CU, Green Choice, City First, Albina, First Green Bank, Green America CC, The Loop CC, Redirect CC, Salmon Nation CC
B	LOCAL CREDIT UNIONS, AFFINITY CCs, TD Bank, American Express, ING
C	MasterCard, Capital One, Sovereign, Santander, Discover, Compass
D	KeyBank, Lloyds Bank, Comerica, Deutsche Bank, RBC, US Bank, VISA, HSBC, RBS, Credit Suisse, UBS
F	Barclay's, Wells Fargo, Morgan Stanley, J.P. Morgan, Chase, Bank of America, Goldman Sachs
X	Citibank

BANKS &
CREDIT CARDS

WHAT YOU NEED TO KNOW
Where you put your money when you're not spending it is just as important as responsibly choosing what you spend it on. For your whole life (even while you sleep), that money will be either building a better world or tearing it down. Small, local banks and credit unions (CU) are typically your best bet. While shopping, make each purchase doubly effective by using a credit card (CC) that donates a percentage of your purchases (over $5,500/yr for the average American) to saving the planet.

BUYING TIPS
✓ Try using both a CU and an 'A' rated bank
✓ Switch to a socially responsible credit card

BEST CHOICE

Amalgamated Bank

☆ B Lab Certified Responsible Company
☆ $15/hr employee minimum wage in 2015
☆ One of the only unionized banks in the US

USEFUL RESOURCES
🖥 www.creditunion.coop/cu_locator
🖥 www.breakupwithyourmegabank.org

BEER

✪	New Belgium
A	Allagash, Alchemist, Aslan, BrewDog, Brewery Vivant, Hopworks, North Coast, Bison, Otter Creek, Redemption Rock, Upslope, Sierra Nevada, Alaskan, Odell, Eel River, Brooklyn, Great Lakes, Full Sail, Maine Beer
B	LOCAL BREWERIES, Aeronaut, Asahi, Anderson Valley, Boulevard, Bell's, Cape Cod, Deschutes, Harpoon, Kona, Long Trail, Ninkasi, Redhook, Stone, Uinta
C	Samuel Smith's, Pabst, Schlitz, Stroh's, Amstel, Heineken, Newcastle, Carlsberg
D	Blue Moon, Coors, Foster's, Guinness, Keystone, Leinenkugel, Miller, Molson, Old Milwaukee, Samuel Adams
F	Beck's, Budweiser, Bass, Busch, Corona, Harp, Lowenbrau, Michelob, Modelo, Natural Light, Rolling Rock, Stella Artois
X	

BEER

BUYING TIPS

✓ Look for B Corp certified breweries
✓ Buy from local microbreweries when possible
✓ Avoid buying beer in plastic bottles

BEST CHOICE

New Belgium

☆ 1st 100% wind-powered brewery
☆ Conserves 50% more water vs. average
☆ An employee-owned business
☆ 4x awarded "Most Democratic Workplace"
☆ $1.6 million donated to local community

BETTER CHOICE

Sierra Nevada

☆ Designated Climate Action Leader
☆ Numerous environmental awards
☆ Recycles 98% of waste created in production

WORSE CHOICE

Budweiser (Anheuser-Busch InBev)

☠ Paid $78 million to Washington lobbyists[12]
☠ EC overall responsibility rating of POOR[30]
☠ US govt sued over monopolistic practices[54]

BIG TECH

★	
A	Wikipedia, Apple, iOS
B	Google, YouTube, Android
C	Snapchat, Zoom, ByteDance, TikTok
D	Pinterest, Reddit, Twitter, Yelp, TenCent, WeChat, Charter
F	Facebook, Meta, Instagram, WhatsApp, Messenger, Amazon, Microsoft, LinkedIn, Skype, Comcast
X	Verizon, Xfinity, Yahoo!, AT&T

BIG TECH

WHAT YOU NEED TO KNOW
This category covers the biggest tech companies worldwide that are increasingly becoming a part of our daily lives. They are growing more powerful every year and must be held more accountable by us.

BETTER CHOICE

Wikipedia

☆ Most utilized nonprofit on the internet
☆ Highly rated for overall neutrality of information
☆ Building infrastructure for info democracy

BETTER CHOICE

Apple

☆ Takes back electronics/computers for recycling
☆ All computers are Energy Star certified
☆ Perfect 100 on HRC Equality Index for nine years

WORST CHOICE

Xfinity (Verizon)

☠ Given $295 million to Washington lobbyists[12]
☠ CEP 'F' for overall social responsibility[14]
☠ Discriminated against pregnant employees[48]

BODY CARE

✪	Dr. Bronner's, Method, EO, Preserve
A	Aveda, Dr. Haushka, Tweezerman, Pangea, Aubrey, Aura Cacia, Badger, Kiss My Face, Tom's of Maine, Auromere, Weleda, Zia, Nubius, Jason, Alba
B	Lush, Ecco Bella, BWC, Body Shop, C.O. Bigleow, Crystal, Colgate, Speed Stick, Mennen, Carmex, Shikai
C	Avalon Organics, Burt's Bees, Nature's Gate, Bic, Blistex, Banana Boat, Schick, Hawaiian Tropic, Edge, Nivea, Dry Idea, Soft & Dri
D	Jergen's, Bioré, Ban, Curel, Unilever, Dove, Axe, Degree, Q-Tips, Suave, Vaseline, Mitchum, Arm & Hammer
F	Coppertone, Keri, Johnson & Johnson, Aveeno, Neutrogena, Lubriderm, Clean & Clear, Purell, Right Guard, Secret, Proctor & Gamble, Noxzema, Oil of Olay, Gillette, Old Spice, Chapstick
X	

BODY CARE

BUYING TIPS

✓ Avoid products tested on animals
✓ Seek out items made with organic ingredients
✓ Look for recyclable containers — #1, #2 plastic
✓ Buy larger quantities to reduce packaging

BETTER CHOICE

Pangea Organics

☆ GAM certified Green Business
☆ Never tests ingredients on animals
☆ 2x award winner for Business Ethics

WORSE CHOICE

Secret (Procter & Gamble)

☠ MM's "Worst Corporation" list for two years[51]
☠ Continues unnecessary animal testing[10]
☠ "Bottom Rung," Ladder of Responsibility[40]
☠ Spent over $68 million on lobbyists[12]

WORST CHOICE

Chapstick (Pfizer)

☠ #64 of PERI 100 Most Toxic Water Polluters[58]
☠ #17 in "Top 100 Corporate Criminals"[51]
☠ MM's "Worst Corporation" list for four years[51]
☠ Paid $221 million to Washington lobbyists[12]

BREAD

✪	LOCAL BAKERY
A	Alvarado St Bakery, Ener-G, Rudi's Organic
B	Great Harvest Bread, Vermont Bread, Food For Life, Sun-Maid
C	Pillsbury, Betty Crocker, Gold Medal, Colombo, Quaker, La Brea, Pepperidge Farm, Wonder Bread, Nature's Pride, Home Pride, Barowsky's, Weight Watchers
D	Arnold, Bimbo, Boboli, Entenmann's, Freihofer's, Oroweat, Thomas' English Muffins, Tia Rosa
F	Alexia, Rainbo, Sara Lee, EarthGrains, Conagra, Lender's
X	Kraft, Stove Top

BREAD

WHAT YOU NEED TO KNOW
Despite all of our technological advancement, it's still a challenge to find a good, socially responsible loaf of bread in the supermarket.

BUYING TIPS
✓ Support a local bakery in your community

BEST CHOICE
Alvarado Street Bakery

☆ Worker-owned cooperative
☆ PC Socially Responsible Business Award
☆ GAM certified Green Business

WORSE CHOICE
Rainbo (Tyson)

☠ CEP 'F' for overall social responsibility[14]
☠ Paid $29 million to Washington lobbyists[12]
☠ MM's "Worst Corporation" list for two years[51]
☠ Violation of Foreign Corrupt Practices Act[71]

USEFUL RESOURCES
🖥 www.cornucopia.org/cereal-scorecard
🖥 www.responsibleshopper.org

BREAKFAST FOOD

✪	**Nature's Path**
A	Tofurkey, Amy's Kitchen
B	Sweet Earth, Gardein, Ian's, Daiya
C	General Mills, Betty Crocker, Pillsbury, Krusteaz, Quaker, Pearl Milling, Entenmann's, Bob Evans, Weight Watchers
D	Smucker's, Hungry Jack, Kellogg's, Eggo, Morningstar Farms, Kashi, Golden Griddle, Skippy, Hormel, Ore-Ida
F	Conagra, Armour, Birds Eye, Log Cabin, Mrs. Butterworth's, Swanson, Banquet, PAM, Tyson, Jimmy Dean
X	**Nestle, Kraft, Nabisco, Boca**

BREAKFAST FOOD

WHAT YOU NEED TO KNOW
Every morning of your life, what you put on your plate for breakfast will determine what kind of world your children inherit in the future.

BUYING TIPS
✓ Buy at least one organic item for breakfast

BEST CHOICE
Nature's Path

☆ GAM certified Green Business
☆ Named one of Canada's Greenest Employers
☆ Sponsors environmental efforts and festivals

BETTER CHOICE
Tofurky (Turtle Island)

☆ EPA Certified 100% Green Power
☆ Highest standards of organic integrity
☆ 1st food sponsor of The Humane Society

WORSE CHOICE
Jimmy Dean (Tyson)

☠ #52 in "Top 100 Corporate Criminals"[51]
☠ Violation of Foreign Corrupt Practices Act[71]
☠ CEP 'F' for overall social responsibility[14]
☠ Paid $29 million to Washington lobbyists[12]

BUTTER & MARGARINE

✪	Organic Valley
A	Miyoko's Creamery, Organic Pastures, Straus Family Creamery, Cabot, Spectrum
B	Earth Balance, Smart Balance, Clover Stornetta
C	Horizon Organic, Canoleo, Kerrygold, Challenge, Saffola, Canola Harvest, Cloverleaf
D	Land O'Lakes, Unilever, Brummel & Brown, I Can't Believe It's Not Butter, Shedd's, Country Crock, Promise, Imperial
F	Conagra, Parkay, Blue Bonnet, Fleischmann's, Johnson & Johnson, Benecol
X	Kraft

BUTTER & MARGARINE

BUYING TIPS

✓ Look for "No Hormones" and "No Antibiotics"
✓ Seek out items made with organic ingredients
✓ Avoid hydrogenated, saturated, and trans fats

BEST CHOICE

Organic Valley

☆ Small family farmer-owned co-operative
☆ Gives 10% of profits to local community
☆ Humane animal treatment a priority
☆ Ranked #3 best company on the planet

WORSE CHOICE

Parkay (Conagra)

☠ #50 in "Top 100 Corporate Criminals"[51]
☠ CEP 'F' for overall social responsibility[14]
☠ CERES "Climate Change Laggard"[15]
☠ Lobbied against GMO labeling[21]

USEFUL RESOURCES

🖳 www.organicconsumers.org
🖳 www.cornucopia.org/dairy_brand_ratings
🖳 www.localharvest.org

CANDY, GUM, & MINTS

✪	
A	Glee Gum, Sencha Naturals, Hain, Speakeasy, St. Claire's Organics
B	Ginger People, Newman's Own, Red Vines
C	Panda, Haribo, La Vie, Tootsie Roll, Andes Mints, Mike & Ike, Mentos, Jelly Belly
D	Tic Tacs, Hershey, Heath, Mounds, Reese's, Kit Kat, Almond Joy, Twizzlers
F	Mars, 3 Musketeers, Big Red, Extra, Life Savers, Orbit, Milky Way, M&M's, Snickers, Skittles, Starburst, Twix, Wrigley's
X	Nestlé, After Eight, Butterfinger, Sweetarts, Wonka, Nerds, Kraft, Certs, Dentyne, Trident, Cadbury

CANDY, GUM, & MINTS

BUYING TIPS
Most major candy manufacturers are also major chocolate purchasers, which currently means that they are using child slave labor to produce much of their candy. It's important to keep these companies accountable until they agree to basic human rights standards in the industry.

BEST CHOICE
Glee Gum

☆ GAM certified Green Business
☆ Uses wild-harvested rainforest plants
☆ Actively supports environmental groups

WORSE CHOICE
M&Ms (Mars)

☠ On MM's "10 Worst Corporations" list[51]
☠ Evidence of involvement in child slave labor[61]
☠ Target of international fair trade campaign[25]
☠ Paid $43 million to Washington lobbyists[12]

USEFUL RESOURCES
💻 www.greenpages.org
💻 www.globalexchange.org

CANNED GOODS

⊛	
A	Eden, Amy's Kitchen, Hain, Westbrae, Bearitos, Native Forest, Muir Glen
B	Ginger People, Sunsweet
C	Santa Cruz Organic, Hamburger Helper, Old El Paso, Progresso, Green Giant, Tree Top, Campbell's, Bush's, Nalley, Ortega, Thai Kitchen, GOYA
D	Ocean Spray, Mott's, Heinz, Del Monte, S&W, Contadina, Hormel, Dinty Moore, Stagg, La Victoria, Unilever, Knorr, Dole, French's
F	Conagra, Dennison's, Hunt's, La Choy, Marie Callender's, Rosarita, Van Camp's
X	Kraft, Libby's, Taco Bell

CANNED GOODS

WHAT YOU NEED TO KNOW
Some of the most socially responsible companies
now provide a wide variety of canned goods that
should be available at most supermarkets.

BEST CHOICE
Eden Foods

☆ Ranked #28 best company on the planet
☆ CEP's highest social responsibility score
☆ GAM certified Green Business

WORST CHOICE
Libby's (Kraft)

☠ Greenwash Award for public deception[25]
☠ Named global climate change laggard[15]
☠ Currently target of two major boycotts[22,55]
☠ Paid $331 million to Washington lobbyists[12]
☠ MM's "Worst Corporation" list for five years[51]

USEFUL RESOURCES
💻 www.responsibleshopper.org
💻 www.ethicalconsumer.org

CARS

★	
A	Honda, Acura, Tesla
B	Hyundai, Kia, Toyota, Lexus, Scion, Subaru
C	Smart, Mini, Volvo, Nissan, Tata, Porsche, Renault, Peugot, BMW, Mazda, Mercedes
D	Ferrari, Isuzu, Volkswagen, Audi, Mitsubishi
F	Ford, Lincoln, Mercury, Chrysler, Fiat, Dodge, Jeep, Jaguar, Land Rover
X	Buick, Cadillac, Chevrolet, General Motors, GMC, Hummer

CARS

BUYING TIPS:
✓ Look for cars/trucks that get at least 30 mpg
✓ Consider a hybrid or fully electric vehicle

BEST CHOICE
Honda
☆ UCS excellent environmental auto ranking
☆ CERES named as climate sustainability leader
☆ Top eco-ranking from Greenopia

WORSE CHOICE
Chrysler
☠ UCS worst environmental auto ranking[69]
☠ Paid $46 million to Washington lobbyists[12]
☠ EC responsibility rating of POOR[30]
☠ $12 billion paid by taxpayers to bailout[54]

WORST CHOICE
General Motors
☠ Leader in fighting clean air legislation[61]
☠ Paid $212 million to Washington lobbyists[12]
☠ MM's "Worst Corporation" list for four years[51]
☠ $31 billion paid by taxpayers to bailout[54]

RESOURCES
🖥 www.fueleconomy.gov

CEREAL

★	**Nature's Path, EnviroKidz**
A	Lydia's Organics, Bob's Red Mill, Alvarado Street, Purely Elizabeth, Barbara's, Health Valley, Earth's Best, Arrowhead Mills, Lundberg, MadeGood
B	Food For Life, Peace Cereal, Cascadian Farm, Newman's Own
C	General Mills, Kix, Pillsbury, Wheaties, Cheerios, Chex, KIND, Total, Nature Valley, Quaker, Mother's, Cream of Wheat, Weight Watchers, Heartland
D	Post, Shredded Wheat, Malt-O-Meal, Grape-Nuts, Kellogg's, Kashi, Corn Flakes, All-Bran, Frosted Flakes, Rice Crispies, Special K, Raisin Bran, Bear Naked
F	
X	Nestlé, Kraft, Back to Nature, Nabisco

CEREAL

WHAT YOU NEED TO KNOW
Currently, choosing a socially responsible cereal is one of the easiest ways to make a difference with your dollars. You'll find many great choices available in most supermarkets.

BEST CHOICE
Nature's Path

☆ GAM certified Green Business
☆ Named one of Canada's Greenest Employers
☆ Sponsors environmental efforts and festivals

BETTER CHOICE
Lydia's Organic

☆ GAM certified Green Business
☆ Does not test on animals
☆ Industry leader in organic integrity

WORST CHOICE
Back To Nature (Kraft)

☠ MM's "Worst Corporation" list for five years[51]
☠ Currently target of two major boycotts[22,55]
☠ Named global climate change laggard[15]

USEFUL RESOURCES
⌨ www.cornucopia.org/cereal-scorecard

CHIPS

★	**Que Pasa**
A	Eden, Barbara's, Late July, Hain Celestial, Bearitos, Garden of Eatin, Terra, Lundberg
B	Kettle Chips
C	Stacy's, Quaker, Food Should Taste Good, Pepperidge Farm, True North, Cape Cod, Mission, Robert's American Gourmet, Utz
D	Cheetos, Doritos, Fritos, Funyuns, Lay's, Ruffles, Sun Chips, Tostitos, Pringles, French's
F	Conagra, Alexia
X	**Kraft, Back to Nature, Nabisco**

CHIPS

BUYING TIPS
✓ Look for chips made with organic ingredients
✓ Avoid hydrogenated, saturated, and trans fats
✓ Buy larger quantities to reduce packaging

BETTER CHOICE
Eden Foods

☆ Ranked #28 best company on the planet
☆ CEP's highest social responsibility score
☆ GAM certified Green Business

WORSE CHOICE
Alexia (Conagra)

☟ MM's "Worst Corporation" list for two years[51]
☟ #50 in "Top 100 Corporate Criminals"[51]
☟ CERES "Climate Change Laggard"[15]

WORST CHOICE
Nabisco (Kraft)

☟ Greenwash Award for public deception[25]
☟ Named global climate change laggard[15]
☟ Currently target of two major boycotts[22,55]
☟ Paid $331 million to Washington lobbyists[12]

USEFUL RESOURCES
🖳 www.responsibleshopper.org

CHOCOLATE

★	**Alter Eco, Equal Exchange, Nutiva**
A	Divine, Theo, Tony's Chocoloney, Endangered Species, SweetRiot, Shaman, Sjaak's, Coco Zen, Rapunzel, Sunspire
B	Sweet Earth, Green & Black's, Lake Champlain, Whittaker's, Terra Nostra, Newman's Own
C	Chocolove, Lindt, Ritter Sport, Ghirardelli, Scharffen Berger
D	Cadbury, Nutella, Ferrero Rocher, Kinder, Godiva, Hershey, Reese's
F	Swiss Miss, 3 Musketeers, Dove, Mars, Milky Way, M&M's, Snickers, Amazon, Happy Belly
X	**Nestlé, Crunch, Ovaltine, Wonka**

CHOCOLATE

WHAT YOU NEED TO KNOW

Recently, the ILO, UNICEF, and US State Department uncovered the widespread use of child slave labor in the chocolate industry — up to 40% of all chocolate is currently being produced in this way.

BUYING TIPS

✓ Companies in the 'A' category are slave-free
✓ Look for chocolate that is fair trade certified
✓ Buy organic chocolate when available

BEST CHOICE

Equal Exchange

☆ GAM certified Green Business
☆ Business Ethics Award winner
☆ Industry leader in fair trade movement
☆ 4x awarded "Most Democratic Workplace"

WORST CHOICE

Crunch (Nestlé)

☠ Aggressive takeovers of family farms[61]
☠ "Most Irresponsible" corporation award[6]
☠ Involved in child slavery lawsuit[61]

USEFUL RESOURCES

www.greenamerica.org

CLEANING PRODUCTS

✪	Seventh Generation, Method, Ecover, Dr. Bronner's
A	Earth Friendly, Biokleen, Air Therapy, Planet, CitraSolv, Mountain Green, EcoLogic, Mrs. Meyers
B	WD-40, Ajax, Murphy's Oil, Shaklee, SC Johnson, Bon Ami, Drano, Fantastik, Glade, Off, Pledge, Scrubbing Bubble, Vanish, Windex
C	Comet, Hefty, Reynolds
D	Arm & Hammer, 3M, Amway, Airwick, Calgon, Chore Boy, Easy-Off, Glass Plus, LimeAway, Lysol, Old English, Spray'n Wash, Wizard, 20 Mule Team Borax, Clorox, Dial, Glad, Green Works, Liquid Plumr, Pine-Sol, SOS, Tilex
F	Endust, Sara Lee, Ty-D-Bol, Procter & Gamble, Dawn, Febreze, Mr. Clean, Swiffer
X	

CLEANING PRODUCTS

BUYING TIPS
✓ Look for nonpetroleum-based products
✓ Avoid products with chlorine/toxic chemicals

BEST CHOICE
Seventh Generation

☆ #3 best company on the planet
☆ Empowers consumers w/packaging
☆ Winner, Sustainability Report Award
☆ Socially Responsible Business Award

BEST CHOICE
Ecover

☆ GAM certified Green Business
☆ Winner, Environmental Leader Award
☆ UN Global 500 Environment Honor Roll
☆ 1st truly ecological factory in the world

WORST CHOICE
Swiffer (Procter & Gamble)

☠ MM's "Worst Corporation" list for two years[51]
☠ Continues unnecessary animal testing[10]
☠ "Bottom Rung," Ladder of Responsibility[40]
☠ Spent over $83 million on lobbyists[12]

CLIMATE CHANGE

★	Electric Car, Home Energy, Plant-Based Diet, Public Transport, Rooftop Solar
A	CleanChoice, Clean Solar, Green Mountain, Mpowered, ReVision, SkyFire, Southern Energy, SunBug Solar, SunCommon, Sun Light & Power, Tesla, TerraPass, ZipCar, Couchsurfing Intl
B	Beyond Meat, Impossible Foods, Suncor, National Grid, Northwest Natural Gas
C	Sunoco, Petro-Canada, Circle K, Costco, Husky, KwikTrip, QuickChek, RaceTrac, Sinclair, Stop N Go, Consolidated Edison
D	Hess, Citgo, Total, Valero, Beacon, Diamond Shamrock, Shamrock, Sempra, Massey, Constellation, Xcel, PG&E
F	76, Unocal, Ashland, Marathon, Speedway, SuperAmerica, Pilot, Flying J, Dominion, Entergy, DTE, Enron, Peabody
X	Southern Co, Duke Energy, Conoco, Phillips 66, Jet, Tosco, Shell, BP, Chevron, Texaco, Exxon, Mobil

CLIMATE CHANGE

WHAT YOU NEED TO KNOW
This may seem an odd choice for a shopping category, but it is so vitally important that we keep this issue at the forefront of our consumption habits that it makes sense to organize some of our major consumer climate change choices in one spot.

BETTER CHOICE

TerraPass

☆ B Lab Certified Responsible Company
☆ GAM Certified Green Business
☆ Most reputable choice for carbon offsets

BETTER CHOICE

ZipCar

☆ GAM Certified Green Business
☆ Offers range of hybrid and electric car choices
☆ Largest car-sharing program in the US

WORST CHOICE

Exxon (Exxon-Mobil)

☠ #21 of Toxic 100 Air Polluters[58]
☠ #35 of Toxic 100 Water Polluters[58]
☠ #11 of Toxic 100 Greenhouse Gas Polluters[58]
☠ One of 12 major companies blocking climate change legislation[44]

CLOTHING

★	**Patagonia**
A	Maggie's Organics, Eileen Fisher, REI, Alta Gracia, Nau, Athleta, Timberland, Levi's
B	GAP, Banana Republic, Old Navy, H&M, Reebok, Adidas, Nike, North Face
C	Gildan, Nicole Miller, American Eagle, Champion, Hanes, Eddie Bauer, Ann Taylor, Benetton, Hugo Boss, Tommy Hilfiger, Calvin Klein, Speedo, Izod, Jockey, Dior, Burlington Coat Factory, Urban Outfitters, Nieman Marcus, L.L. Bean, J Crew
D	Lululemon, Carter's, Under Armour, FILA, Abercrombie, Esprit, Kenneth Cole, Vans, Bill Blass, Russell, Perry Ellis, Guess, DKNY, Land's End, Saks, Kohl's, Jones, Skechers, Dick's, Lord & Taylor, Ross, Forever 21, Wrangler, Lee, VF, JC Penney, Kmart
F	Victoria's Secret, Limited, PINK, Express, Marshall's, T.J. Maxx, Target, Hudson's, Costco, Fruit of the Loom, Dillard's, Macy's, Ralph Lauren, Disney, Amazon
X	**Walmart**

CLOTHING

WHAT YOU NEED TO KNOW
The fact is that many of the clothes we wear today are made in sweatshops in the developing world. Better companies have either US-made clothing or strictly enforced human rights standards that ensure fair wages and safe working conditions.

BETTER CHOICE
Maggie's Organics

☆ Socially Responsible Business Award
☆ Industry leader in fair trade movement
☆ GAM "Top Rung," Ladder of Responsibility
☆ GAM certified Green Business

WORSE CHOICE
Macy's

☠ Weak code of conduct for sweatshops[14]
☠ RS 'F' for overall social responsibility[61]
☠ Named "Sweatshop Laggard" by CEP[14]
☠ "Bottom Rung," Ladder of Responsibility[40]

USEFUL RESOURCES
🖳 www.cleanclothes.org
🖳 en.maquilasolidarity.org
🖳 www.free2work.org
🖳 www.labourbehindthelabel.org

COFFEE

⭐	**Equal Exchange, Grounds for Change**
A	Moka Joe, Higher Grounds, Pura Vida, Peace Coffee, Cafe Campesino, Dean's Beans, Jim's, Thanksgiving, Wicked Joe, Cafe Mam, Larry's, ethical bean, Caffe Ibis
B	LOCAL COFFEE SHOPS
C	Starbucks, Alterra, illy, Allegro, Caribou, Green Mountain, Peet's, Seattle's Best, La Colombe, Lavazza, Eight O'Clock, Hills Bros, Gevalia
D	Continental, International Delight
F	Amazon, Solimo
X	Nestlé, Nespresso, Sanka, CoffeeMate, Kraft, Mondelez, Folgers, Maxwell House, General Foods, Yuban, Sanka

COFFEE

WHAT YOU NEED TO KNOW
Global coffee prices have plummeted recently, pushing some coffee farmers in the developing world to the brink of starvation. Buying fair trade coffee is now more important than ever.

BUYING TIPS
✓ Look for fair trade, shade grown, organic
✓ Support local, independent coffee shops

BEST CHOICE
Equal Exchange

☆ 4x Awarded "Most Democratic Workplace"
☆ Worker-owned cooperative
☆ B Lab & GAM Certified Responsible Company
☆ Industry leader in fair trade movement
☆ Fair trade, organic, shade-grown coffee

WORST CHOICE
Nespresso (Nestlé)

☠ Involved in union busting outside US[61]
☠ "Bottom Rung," Ladder of Responsibility[40]
☠ Aggressive takeovers of family farms[61]
☠ Baby formula human rights boycott[48]

USEFUL RESOURCES
💻 www.transfairusa.org

COMPUTERS & ACCESSORIES

✪	
A	HP, Apple, Cisco, Intel
B	Google, Dell, Sun, AMD, Canon, Adobe, Lexmark
C	IBM, NEC, Packard Bell, Intuit, Seagate, nVidia, Umax, Seagate, Logitech, Brother, Sandisk, Imation, 3Com, Seiko, Epson, Best Buy, Western Digital, Belkin, Asus, NCR, Maxell, Micron
D	Sony, Toshiba, Fujitsu, Viewsonic, AST, Lenovo, LG, Hitachi, Vizio, Philips, Panasonic, Acer, Sharp, Samsung
F	Amazon, Oracle, Peoplesoft, Microsoft
X	GE

COMPUTERS & ACCESSORIES

WHAT YOU NEED TO KNOW
Computers have become an essential part of every-day life for many of us, but that need to stay up to date has also led to a rapidly growing problem of toxic computer waste in our landfills.

BEST CHOICE
HP (Hewlett Packard)

☆ Free return recycling of its computers
☆ Perfect 100 on HRC Equality Index
☆ Countless awards for business ethics

WORSE CHOICE
Microsoft

☠ RS 'F' for overall social responsibility[40]
☠ Named "abusive monopoly" by US Court[48]
☠ Paid $193 million to Washington lobbyists[12]
☠ Greenpeace "Green Electronics Laggard"[44]
☠ Refuses disclosure on its business[14]

USEFUL RESOURCES
🖥 www.greenpeace.org/greenerelectronics
🖥 www.electronicstakeback.com
🖥 www.svtc.org

CONDIMENTS & DRESSINGS

✪	Nature's Path
A	Eden, Annie's, Sir Kensington's, San-J, Sierra Nevada, Follow Your Heart, Vegenaise, Hain Celestial, Westbrae, Spectrum
B	Ginger People, Nasoya, Woodstock Farms, OrganicVille, Bragg
C	Pepperidge Farm, Mrs. Dash, Sriracha (Huy Fong), Tabasco, Tapatio, Kikkoman, Thai Kitchen
D	Best Foods, Knorr, Lizano, McCormick, Lawry's, Old Bay, Del Monte, Contadina, La Victoria, Heinz, TGI Fridays, Lea & Perrins, Jack Daniels, French's, Hidden Valley, KC Masterpiece
F	Gulden's, Hunt's, La Choy, Con Agra, Wish-Bone
X	Kraft, A1, Bull's-Eye, Good Seasons, Grey Poupon, Miracle Whip

CONDIMENTS & DRESSINGS

WHAT YOU NEED TO KNOW
Whether you're looking for ketchup, mustard, mayonnaise, soy sauce, or salad dressing, there are now socially responsible brands of each.

BETTER CHOICE
Eden Foods

☆ Ranked #28 best company on the planet
☆ CEP's highest social responsibility score
☆ Top rated for its organic integrity

BETTER CHOICE
Sierra Nevada

☆ Designated Climate Action Leader
☆ Numerous environmental awards
☆ Recycles 98% of waste created in production

WORST CHOICE
Miracle Whip (Kraft)

☠ Named "Top 10 Greenwasher"[48]
☠ Paid $329 million to Washington lobbyists[12]
☠ Involved in document deletion cover-up[48]

COOKIES & CRACKERS

✪	**Nature's Path**
A	Lydia's Organic, Mary's Gone Crackers, Annie's, San-J, Barbara's, Edward & Sons, Late July, Doctor Kracker, Hain Celestial, Earth's Best, Health Valley, Lundberg
B	Immaculate Baking Co, Newman's Own, Cascadian Farm
C	Quaker, Mother's, Pepperidge Farm, LU, MI-DEL, Mrs. Field's, Ryvita, Wasa, RyKrisp
D	Kellogg's, Famous Amos, Kashi, Keebler, Sunshine
F	Amazon, Happy Belly
X	**Kraft, Back to Nature, Nabisco, SnackWell's**

COOKIES & CRACKERS

WHAT YOU NEED TO KNOW
The socially responsible cookie industry has recently exploded, so there's no longer any need to feel guilty about reaching into the cookie jar.

BEST CHOICE
Nature's Path

☆ GAM certified Green Business
☆ Named one of Canada's Greenest Employers
☆ Sponsors environmental efforts and festivals

BETTER CHOICE
Lydia's Organic

☆ GAM certified Green Business
☆ Does not test on animals
☆ Industry leader in organic integrity

WORST CHOICE
Nabisco (Kraft)

☠ Part of #2 worst company on the Earth[10]
☠ Currently the target of 2 major boycotts[22,55]
☠ Spent over $331 million on lobbyists[12]
☠ Greenwash Award for public deception[48]

COSMETICS

⭐	Dr. Bronner's, ECO Lips, EO
A	Aveda, Dr. Haushka, Tweezerman, Pangea, Aubrey, Aura Cacia, Badger, Kiss My Face, Auromere, Weleda, Beautycounter, Ethique
B	Alba, Jason, Lush, The Body Shop, Avon, Ecco Bella, BWC, C.O. Bigleow, Physician's Formula, Paul Penders, Freeman
C	Avalon Organics, Burt's Bees, Nature's Gate, Blistex, CoverGirl, Nivea, Wet n Wild
D	Sephora, Helene Curtis, L'Oreal, Lancôme, Maybelline, Pureology, Jergen's, Bioré, Melaleuca, Revlon, Almay, Clinique, Estée Lauder
F	Amazon, Johnson & Johnson, Aveeno, Neutrogena, Max Factor, Noxzema, Oil of Olay
X	

COSMETICS

WHAT YOU NEED TO KNOW
While some cosmetics companies still carry out tests on animals, many smaller companies now provide animal- and eco-friendly alternatives.

BUYING TIPS
✓ Choose companies that don't test on animals
✓ Look for products with organic ingredients

BEST CHOICE
EO

☆ Products never tested on animals
☆ GAM certified Green Business
☆ B Lab Certified Responsible Company
☆ Containers made from recycled PET bottles

WORST CHOICE
Max Factor (Procter & Gamble)

☣ Continues unnecessary animal testing[10]
☣ "Bottom Rung," Ladder of Responsibility[40]
☣ MM's "Worst Corporation" list for two years[51]
☣ Spent over $83 million on lobbyists[12]

USEFUL RESOURCES
🖳 www.caringconsumer.org
🖳 www.ewg.org

DAIRY ALTERNATIVES

★	**Organic Valley**
A	Nancy's, Eden, So Delicious, Wildwood, Miyoko's, Ripple, VitaCoco, Follow Your Heart, WestSoy
B	Pacific, 365, Almond Breeze, Blue Diamond, Califia, Earth/Smart Balance, Forager, GoodKarma, JUST, Kite Hill, Malk, Milkadamia, Mooala, NotMilk, Nutpods, Oatly, Orgain, Planet Oat, Tempt, Tofutti, Treeline, ZenSoy, VitaSoy, Silk
C	Chobani, Siggi's, Soyco, Soymage
D	Soy/Rice/Almond Dream, 8th Continent
F	Amazon, Happy Belly
X	**Kraft, Cool Whip, Nestlé, Carnation**

DAIRY ALTERNATIVES

BUYING TIPS
✓ Choose organic products when available
✓ Look for items with easily recycled containers

BEST CHOICE
Organic Valley

☆ Largest US cooperative of small family farms
☆ Top rated for its organic integrity
☆ Multiple responsible business awards

BETTER CHOICE
Nancy's

☆ Largely solar-powered workplace
☆ GAM certified Green Business
☆ 2x Socially Responsible Business Awards

WORST CHOICE
Cool Whip (Kraft)

☠ Currently target of two major boycotts[22,55]
☠ #4 contributor to Washington lobbyists[12]
☠ Involved in document deletion cover-up[48]

USEFUL RESOURCES
🖥 www.organicconsumers.org
🖥 www.cornucopia.org/soysurvey

DAIRY PRODUCTS

★	Organic Valley
A	Nancy's, Redwood Hill, Organic Pastures, Brown Cow, Cabot, Tillamook, Helios, Stonyfield, Clover, Straus Family Creamery
B	Lifeway, Kevita, Wallaby, Green Valley, Smari, Dannon
C	Athenos, Chobani, Daisy, Hood, Horizon, Kerrygold, Lucerne, President, Rondele, Sargento, Siggi's, Weight Watchers
D	Borden, Kozy Shack, Land O'Lakes, Laughing Cow
F	Hunt's, Reddi-wip, Lactaid, Sara Lee, Continental, International Delight, Alta Dena, Berkeley Farms, Borden, Dairy Ease, Garelick Farms, Mayfield, Meadow Gold, PET, Amazon, Happy Belly
X	Nestlé, Carnation, Kraft, Cool Whip, Cracker Barrel, Jell-O, Knudsen, Philadelphia Cream Cheese, Velveeta

DAIRY PRODUCTS

WHAT YOU NEED TO KNOW
While large corporate farms are the norm for the dairy industry, many small family farms are fighting back by going organic in order to survive.

BUYING TIPS
✓ Look for "No Hormones" and "No Antibiotics"
✓ Choose items made with organic ingredients

BEST CHOICE
Organic Valley

☆ Largest US cooperative of small family farms
☆ Top rated for its organic integrity
☆ Multiple responsible business awards

WORST CHOICE
Cracker Barrel (Kraft)

☠ Part of #2 worst company on the Earth[4]
☠ Currently the target of 2 major boycotts[22,55]
☠ Greenwashing Award for public deception[48]
☠ Named global climate change laggard[15]
☠ Named "Top 10 Greenwasher"[48]

USEFUL RESOURCES
🖥 www.organicconsumers.org
🖥 www.cornucopia.org/dairy_brand_ratings

DENTAL CARE

★	Preserve
A	Tom's of Maine, Kiss My Face, Auromere, Jäsön, Weleda
B	EcoDent, Colgate, Ultrabrite, NOW
C	Nature's Gate, Burt's Bees
D	Unilever, Pepsodent, Church & Dwight, Aim, Arm & Hammer, Mentadent
F	Johnson & Johnson, Listerine, Reach, Rembrandt, Aquafresh, Fixodent, Anbesol, ACT, GlaxoSmithKline, Polident, Poligrip, Abreva, Procter & Gamble, Crest, Oral-B, Scope, Sensodyne
X	

DENTAL CARE

WHAT YOU NEED TO KNOW
Smaller environmentally friendly companies now offer increasingly popular alternatives to the dental products of larger mainstream corporations.

BUYING TIPS
✓ Buy products made with recycled content
✓ Buy items with easily recycled packaging

BEST CHOICE
Preserve (Recycline)

☆ Environmental leader in industry
☆ Products from 100% recycled plastic
☆ Take-back recycling of all products

WORSE CHOICE
Aquafresh (GlaxoSmithKline)

☠ MM's "Worst Corporation" list for two years[51]
☠ CEP "F" for overall social responsibility[14]
☠ Paid $86 million to Washington lobbyists[12]

WORST CHOICE
Crest (Procter & Gamble)

☠ GAM "Bottom Rung," responsibility rating[40]
☠ NRDC named "environmental laggard"[53]
☠ Paid $106 million to Washington lobbyists[12]

EGGS

✪	Organic Valley
A	Pete & Gerry's, Alexandre Kids, Burroughs Family, Keedysville Valley, Lazy 69, Old Friends, Organic Pastures, Redhill Farms, St. John Family, Stony Brook Valley, World's Best Eggs
B	Wilcox, Farmers' Hen House, Nature's Yolk, Schultz's Eggs, Shenandoah Valley, Vital Farms, Alderfer Eggs, Blue Sky Family, Born Free, Egg Innovations, Giving Nature, Happy Egg, Clover, Trader Joe's
C	Horizon Organic, O Organics, The Country Hen, Archer Farms, Eggology, Giroux Poultry, Judy's Family Farm, Nest Fresh
D	Decoster, Eggland's Best, Lucerne
F	Egg Beaters
X	

EGGS

WHAT YOU NEED TO KNOW
Factory farming has made egg production today a
cruel and environmentally damaging endeavor.
Seek out smaller, more humane options.

BUYING TIPS
✓ Look for cage-free or free-range eggs
✓ Buy organic eggs whenever possible
✓ Seek out local farmers markets

BETTER CHOICE
Pete & Gerry's

☆ B Lab Certified Responsible Company
☆ Supports sustainable family farms
☆ First Certified Humane US egg producer

WORST CHOICE
EggBeaters (Conagra)

☠ Involved in major accounting scandal[73]
☠ 2nd largest E. coli meat recall in history[55]
☠ Many worker safety & health violations[61]

USEFUL RESOURCES
🖳 www.cornucopia.org/organic-egg-scorecard
🖳 www.certifiedhumane.org

ELECTRONICS

★	
A	Apple
B	Google, Kodak, Texas Instruments, Canon, Konica, Minolta, Conair, Norelco
C	Best Buy, Garmin, Koss, Nikon, Plantronics, Sennheiser, Haier, Energizer, Eveready, Kenwood, Aiwa, Coby, TDK, Grundig, Pentax, Rayovac, Polaroid, Bosch
D	HTC, Fry's, RCA, Fuji, Sanyo, Arrow, Radio Shack, Fujitsu, Viewsonic, Toshiba, JVC, Samsung, Sony, Vizio, Huawei, ZTE, 3M, Daewoo, Vivo, Philips, Panasonic, LG, Sharp, Emerson, Acer, Mitsubishi
F	Nintendo, Amazon, Duracell, Microsoft
X	GE

ELECTRONICS

WHAT YOU NEED TO KNOW
Our addiction to the latest electronics has created a significant drain on our energy grid (even when they're off!) as well as a major recycling problem.

BUYING TIPS
✓ Look for electronics with Energy Star labels
✓ Buy rechargeable (NiMH) batteries
✓ Choose electronics that are recyclable

BEST CHOICE

Apple

☆ Takes back electronics/computers for recycling
☆ All computers are Energy Star certified
☆ Perfect 100 on HRC Equality Index for nine years

WORST CHOICE

GE (General Electric)

☠ MM's "Worst Corporation" list for five years[51]
☠ Responsible for 116 toxic Superfund sites[61]
☠ #1 contributor to Washington lobbyists[12]
☠ #4 of PERI 100 Most Toxic Air Polluters[58]

USEFUL RESOURCES
🖥 www.electronicstakeback.com
🖥 www.svtc.org

ENERGY

⊛	
A	3 Phases, Bullfrog Power, CleanChoice, Clean Solar, Creative Energies, Encore, Green Mountain, Mpowered, ReVision, SkyFire, Southern Energy, SunBug Solar, SunCommon, Sun Light & Power
B	Suncor, National Grid, Northwest Natural
C	Cinergy, AEP, WGL, Oneok, XTO, Energen, Cimarex, Washington Gas & Light, Cascade NG, Southern CA Edison, Reliant, Baltimore, Consolidated Edison
D	Aquila, Detroit Edison, Baldor, Sempra, Massey, Constellation, Consol, Arch Coal, Calpine, Rio Tinto, Xcel, PPL, PG&E, Allegheny, Exelon
F	Dominion, Entergy, DTE, Enron, Edison Intl, Peabody, First, American Electric
X	Southern Co, Duke Energy

ENERGY

WHAT YOU NEED TO KNOW
This category covers the biggest tech companies worldwide that are increasingly becoming a part of our daily lives. They are growing more powerful every year and must be held more accountable by us.

BETTER CHOICE

3 Phases Renewables

☆ B Lab Certified Responsible Company
☆ EPA Green-E Certified Company
☆ Supplies clean energy to many companies/govts

WORST CHOICE

Southern Company

☠ #2 of PERI 100 Most Greenhouse Gas Polluters[58]
☠ #12 of PERI 100 Toxic Water Polluters[58]
☠ Paid $251 million to Washington lobbyists[12]

WORST CHOICE

Duke Energy

☠ Rated 'F' (2/100) for clean energy commitment[64]
☠ #2 of PERI 100 Most Greenhouse Gas Polluters[58]
☠ Paid $2.6 billion in fines for violating environmental, manipulation, and employment laws[77]

ENERGY BARS

★	Patagonia, Alpsnack, Nature's Path, Nutiva
A	CLIF, Luna, Z Bar, Urban Remedy, ALOHA, Real Food Bar, The GFB, OLLY, Your Super, Kuli Kuli, Annie's, MadeGood
B	BumbleBar, nomz, Health Valley, ProBar, Kate's Real Food, Bobo's, Vega
C	General Mills, LÄRABAR, FiberOne, Nature Valley, Bulletproof, KIND, Nature's Bakery, GU, Skratch, That's it, Think!, IQ Bar, Huel, Zing, GoMacro, Picky Rise, Raw Rev, Orgain, Power Crunch, Quaker, Gatorade, Stinger, Atkins, Quest, Weight Watchers, Quantum
D	Oatmega, Kellogg's, Kashi, Nutrigrain, RxBar, Slim Fast, Tiger's Milk
F	Kirkland, Kudos, Wickedly Prime
X	Zone, PowerBar, Balance, MET-Rx, Planter's, Perfect Bar, Pure Protein, Best Bar Ever, South Beach

ENERGY BARS

WHAT YOU NEED TO KNOW
Because many energy bar companies have truly
stepped up to the plate, your choice of energy bar
is one of the easiest ways to make a powerful difference for people and the planet.

BEST CHOICE
Nature's Path

☆ GAM certified Green Business
☆ Named one of Canada's Greenest Employers
☆ Sponsors environmental efforts and festivals

BETTER CHOICE
CLIF

☆ Winner, Business Ethics Award
☆ EPA Green Power Leader award winner
☆ #22 best company on the Earth

WORST CHOICE
Balance (Kraft)

☠ Part of #2 worst company on the Earth[4]
☠ Named global climate change laggard[15]
☠ Named "Top 10 Greenwasher"[48]
☠ #4 top contributor to Washington lobbyists[12]

ENERGY DRINKS

⊛	Guayaki
A	CLIF, Honest Tea, Adina, Sambazon, Runa
B	Steaz
C	Starbucks, 5-Hour Energy, Red Bull, Hansen's, Monster, Full Throttle
D	Snapple, AriZona, Rockstar, Jones, Lipton, Recharge, SoBe, Propel, AMP, Muscle Milk, Gatorade, Slim Fast, Special K
F	Vitamin Water, Powerade, Fuze, Vault, Tab, Glaceau, BPM
X	Boost, Ensure

ENERGY DRINKS

WHAT YOU NEED TO KNOW
Just in the past two years have socially responsible
choices for energy drinks finally become available.
It's important to support these options wherever
you find them.

BUYING TIPS
✓ Buy drinks in aluminum or glass containers

BEST CHOICE
Guayaki

☆ Organic, fair trade certified products
☆ Uses sustainably harvested rainforest plants
☆ 3x Awarded "Most Democratic Workplace"
☆ GAM certified Green Business

WORSE CHOICE
Powerade (Coca-Cola)

☠ MM's "Worst Corporation" list for three years[51]
☠ CAI hinders clean water access abroad[22]
☠ Target of major human rights boycotts[30]
☠ Paid $101 million to Washington lobbyists[12]

USEFUL RESOURCES
🖥 www.opensecrets.org
🖥 www.stopcorporateabuse.org
🖥 www.multinationalmonitor.org

FAST FOOD

★	
A	Native Foods, HipCityVeg, Plant Power, Amy's Drive Thru, NextLevel, PLNT Burger, Meta Burger, Project Pollo, Slutty Vegan, Veggie Grill, Mas Veggies, Boloco
B	Burgerville, Pizza Fusion, B.Good, EVOS, Chipotle, Noodles & Company, LarkBurger
C	Panera, In-N-Out, Einstein Bros, Boston Market, Moe's, Carraba's, Ruby Tuesday's, Shoney's, Red Robin, Popeye's, Papa John's, Quiznos, Panda Express, Chuck E. Cheese, Bob Evans, Tim Hortons
D	Subway, TGI Fridays, Applebee's, Dunkin, Buffalo Wild Wings, IHOP, Little Caeser, DQ, Red Lobster, Olive Garden, Jack In The Box, Carl's Jr, Hardee's, Chik-fil-A, Chili's, Outback, Cracker Barrel, QDoba
F	McDonald's, Burger King, Domino's, KFC, Taco Bell, Pizza Hut, Wendy's, Arby's, Long John Silver, Baja Fresh, A&W
X	

FAST FOOD & RESTAURANTS

WHAT YOU NEED TO KNOW
The overall picture of the highly competitive fast-food industry is not a pretty one, but if you find yourself in a pinch, there are a handful of companies to choose from that are on the cutting edge of responsibility. Support them whenever possible and let them know that you appreciate their efforts.

BETTER CHOICE
Boloco

☆ Certified Green Restaurant
☆ 100% transparency for ingredients/sources
☆ B Lab Certified Responsible Company

WORST CHOICE
KFC (Kentucky Fried Chicken)

☠ Linked to rainforest destruction abroad[44]
☠ Involved with plastic toy sweatshops[61]
☠ Target of major consumer boycott[30]
☠ Evidence of false nutritional claims[61]

USEFUL RESOURCES
🖥 www.cspinet.org
🖥 www.responsibleshopper.org

FEMININE CARE

✪	Seventh Generation, Gladrags, Luna Pads
A	The Keeper, Moon Cup, Diva Cup, Organic Essentials, Natracare, Maxim
B	Kotex, Poise
C	Playtex, ClearBlue, Summer's Ever, EPT, Vagisil, Massengil
D	First Response
F	Stayfree, O.B., CareFree, Tampax, Always
X	

FEMININE CARE

WHAT YOU NEED TO KNOW
Much of the effort for socially responsible business
has been driven by women, so it's not surprising
that there are many great options in this category.

BUYING TIPS
✓ Buy care products with less packaging waste

BEST CHOICE
Seventh Generation

☆ Ranked #3 best company on the planet
☆ Empowers consumers w/packaging
☆ Socially Responsible Business Award

BEST CHOICE
Luna Pads

☆ GAM certified Green Business
☆ B Lab Certified Responsible Company
☆ EC overall responsibility rating of GOOD

WORST CHOICE
Tampax (Procter & Gamble)

☠ MM's "Worst Corporation" list for two years[51]
☠ Continues unnecessary animal testing[10]
☠ Target of major consumer boycott[30]

FROZEN DINNERS

⊛	
A	Amy's Kitchen, Annie's, Tofurkey, Ethnic Gourmet, Linda McCartney, Rising Moon
B	Sweet Earth, Ian's, Daiya, Applegate Farms, Cascadian Farms, Newman's Own
C	General Mills, Totino's, Foster Farms, Seeds of Change, Claim Jumper, Michelina's, Tony's, Michael Angelo's, Gorton's, Health Is Wealth, Ling Ling, Lean Gourmet, Freschetta, Red Baron, Quorn, Weight Watchers
D	Kraft-Heinz, Bagel Bites, Boston Market, Ore-Ida, Smart Ones, TGI Friday's, Kashi, Kellogg's, Morningstar Farms, Hormel
F	Conagra, Alexia, Banquet, Bertolli, Birds Eye, Gardein, Hungry Man, Healthy Choice, Marie Callender's, Swanson, Van de Kamps, Ben's Original, Smithfield, Armour, Tyson, Jimmy Dean
X	Nestlé, Hot Pockets, Lean Cuisine, Stouffer's, Sweet Earth, Kraft, Nabisco, Boca

FROZEN DINNERS

WHAT YOU NEED TO KNOW
Today's stress-filled lifestyles have created
increasing demand for quick and easy meals. Luck-
ily, a number of responsible companies have de-
cided to focus on options that are good for people
and the planet.

BEST CHOICE
Amy's Kitchen

☆ Donates food to relief efforts
☆ Produces all-vegetarian organic foods
☆ GAM certified Green Business

WORSE CHOICE
Ben's Original (Mars)

☠ On MM's "10 Worst Corporations" list[51]
☠ Evidence of involvement in child slave labor[61]
☠ Target of international fair trade campaign[25]
☠ Paid $43 million to Washington lobbyists[12]

WORST CHOICE
Lean Cuisine (Nestlé)

☠ Baby formula human rights boycott[48]
☠ "Most Irresponsible" corporation award[6]
☠ Aggressive takeovers of family farms[61]
☠ Involved in union busting outside US[61]

FRUITS & VEGETABLES

⭐	**LOCAL FARMERS MARKETS, CSAs, Equal Exchange**
A	Earthbound Farm, Olivia's, Stahlbush, Cal-Organic, Bunny Luv, Grimmway Farms, Organic Girl, Woodstock Farms
B	Herb Thyme, Pure Pacific, Cascadian Farm, Newman's Own, Ian's, Sunsweet, Sunkist, Sun-Maid
C	General Mills, Green Giant, Birds Eye, Ready Pac, Salad Time, Flav-R-Pac
D	Ocean Spray, Pepsi, Tropicana, Del Monte, Ore-Ida, Dole, Hidden Valley, Fresh Express
F	Conagra, Alexia, C&W
X	

FRUIT & VEGETABLES

WHAT YOU NEED TO KNOW
Fresh produce is the vanguard of the organic foods movement. It's particularly important to buy local produce, so attend your local farmers market or join a CSA (community supported agriculture) farm.

BEST CHOICE
Equal Exchange

☆ 4x Awarded "Most Democratic Workplace"
☆ Worker-owned cooperative
☆ B Lab & GAM Certified Responsible Company
☆ Industry leader in fair trade movement

WORSE CHOICE
Fresh Express (Chiquita)

☠ MM's "Worst Corporation" list for two years[51]
☠ Hired Colombian criminals to protect crops[48]
☠ EC overall responsibility rating of POOR[30]
☠ Evaded taxes using offshore bank accounts[61]

USEFUL RESOURCES
⌨ www.localharvest.org
⌨ www.farmfresh.org

GASOLINE

★	
A	
B	
C	Sunoco, Petro Canada, Circle K, Costco, Husky, KwikTrip, QuickChek, RaceTrac, Sinclair, Stop N Go
D	Hess, Apache, CITGO, Total, Valero, Beacon, Diamond Shamrock, Shamrock, Ultramar
F	76, Unocal, Ashland, Marathon, Speedway, SuperAmerica, Pilot, Flying J
X	Conoco, Phillips 66, Jet, Superclean Tosco, Shell, BP, Chevron, Texaco, Exxon-Mobil

GASOLINE

WHAT YOU NEED TO KNOW

The petroleum industry is one of the least socially and environmentally responsible on the planet, so if you don't want to get your hands dirty, you should sell your car. For the rest of us, it's very important to avoid the companies at the bottom of this category as they are some of the most destructive in existence. If you can manage it, go electric!

BUYING TIPS

✓ Locate the best-ranked gas station near your home and work

BETTER CHOICE

Sunoco

☆ Most eco-friendly refineries in industry

☆ Only oil signatory to CERES Principles

☆ 1st company to recognize climate change

WORST CHOICE

ExxonMobil

☠ #1 worst corporation on the planet[4]

☠ Repeated violator of human rights[61]

☠ #5 in "Top 100 Corporate Criminals"[51]

☠ Paid $289 million to Washington lobbyists[12]

☠ Only negative score ever given by HRC[46]

☠ Extensive record of environmental damage[48]

HAIR CARE

✪	**Dr. Bronner's, EO**
A	Aveda, Dr. Haushka, Aubrey, Aura Cacia, Badger, Druide, Kiss My Face, Tom's of Maine, Weleda, Zia, Nubius, Jason, Alba
B	Lush, Ecco Bella, BWC, The Body Shop, Citre Shine, Paul Mitchell, Paul Penders, Pure & Basic, Pureology, Shikai
C	Avalon Organics, Burt's Bees, Nature's Gate, Giovanni, Desert Essence, Joico
D	Finesse, Biolage, Matrix, Unilever, Dove, Axe, Nexxus, St. Ives, Suave, Sunsilk, Tresemme, V05
F	Johnson & Johnson, Aveeno, Neutrogena, Rogaine, Proctor & Gamble, Aussie, Head & Shoulders, Herbal Essences, Ivory, Pert, Pantene, Vidal Sassoon, Selsun Blue, Clairol
X	

HAIR CARE

BUYING TIPS
✓ Avoid products tested on animals
✓ Seek out items made with organic ingredients
✓ Buy recyclable containers: #1, #2 plastic
✓ Buy larger quantities to reduce packaging

BETTER CHOICE

Druide

☆ 100% sustainably harvested ingredients
☆ Uses strict ECOCERT organic standards
☆ Fair trade, organic ingredients
☆ Industry leader in environment category

WORST CHOICE

Neutrogena (Johnson & Johnson)

☠ Violation of Foreign Corrupt Practices Act[71]
☠ RS 'F' for overall social responsibility[61]
☠ MM's "Worst Corporation" list[51]
☠ Paid $129 million to Washington lobbyists[12]

WORST CHOICE

Revlon

☠ CEP 'F' for overall social responsibility[14]
☠ Continues unnecessary animal testing[10]
☠ Refuses disclosure to consumers[14]

HOTELS

★	
A	Adrift, Artiem, Qbic, Couchsurfing Intl, Kimpton Hotels
B	Marriott, Courtyard, Ritz Carlton, Bulgari, Renaissance, Saunders, Hyatt
C	Wyndham, Ramada, Super 8, Days Inn, Howard Johnson, Motel 6, Novotel, Sofitel, Red Roof Inn, Westin, Knights Inn, Hawthorn, Harrah's, Comfort Inn/Suites, Econo Lodge, Quality Inn, Radisson, Clarion, Hotels.com, Best Western, La Quinta, Sheraton, Westin, Starwood, Crowne Plaza, Express, Holiday Inn, Carlson, Travelodge
D	MGM, Mirage, Hilton, DoubleTree, Conrad, Embassy, Hampton Inn
F	
X	

HOTELS

WHAT YOU NEED TO KNOW
Whether for business or pleasure, choosing where you stay can have a greater impact than even how you travel there and back.

BUYING TIPS
✓ Whenever possible, stay in a locally owned inn, bed & breakfast, or international hostel

BETTER CHOICE
Kimpton Hotels

☆ Environmental leader in the hotel industry
☆ Perfect 100 on HRC Equality Index
☆ Green Seal certified green lodging
☆ GAM certified Green Business

WORSE CHOICE
Hilton Hotels

☠ Rated "Very Poor" by Ethical Consumer[30]
☠ CC foot dragging on climate change efforts[30]
☠ Paid $55 million to Washington lobbyists[12]

USEFUL RESOURCES
💻 www.greenhotels.com
💻 www.sustainabletravel.org
💻 www.tripadvisor.com/GreenLeaders

ICE CREAM & FROZEN DESSERTS

✪	
A	Straus Family Creamery, Tillamook, Jeni's, Stonyfield Farm, Blue Marble, Peekaboo, So Delicious, Clover, Ben & Jerry's
B	Ciao Bella, Coconut Bliss, Alden's Organic, Julie's Organic, Three Twins, Boulder, Oatly, Newman's Own
C	Starbucks, Pillsbury, Hood, Lucerne, Tofutti, Dr. Oetker, Pepperidge Farm, Weight Watchers
D	Almond/Rice/Soy Dream, Hershey, Godiva, Unilever, Klondike, Breyers, Good Humor
F	Conagra, Marie Callender's, Reddi Wip, Mars, Dove, Snickers, Sara Lee
X	Nestlé, Carnation, Dreyer's, Skinny Cow, Häagen-Dazs, Edy's, Kraft, Cool Whip

ICE CREAM & FROZEN DESSERTS

BUYING TIPS
✓ Choose ice cream with organic ingredients
✓ Look for fair trade coffee/chocolate flavors

BEST CHOICE
Straus Family

☆ 1st 100% organic dairy in US
☆ Uses returnable glass bottles for milk
☆ Utilizes methane capture for waste
☆ Small, sustainable family farm

WORST CHOICE
Dreyer's (Nestlé)

☠ Baby formula human rights boycott[48]
☠ "Most Irresponsible" corporation award[6]
☠ Involved in child slavery lawsuit[61]
☠ Aggressive takeovers of family farms[61]

WORST CHOICE
Snickers (Mars)

☠ On MM's "10 Worst Corporations" list[51]
☠ Evidence of involvement in child slave labor[61]
☠ Target of international fair trade campaign[25]
☠ Paid $43 million to Washington lobbyists[12]

INSURANCE COMPANIES

★	Better World Club
A	
B	Kaiser, Nationwide, TIAA-CREF, Progressive
C	Principal Financial, Esurance, Travelers, Pacific Life, UnumProvident, USAA, AAA, Amica, Harvard Pilgrim, Humana, Mutual of Omaha, Capital One, Safeco, Catholic Healthcare, Chubb, American Family, Humana
D	Cigna, Aetna, MetLife, United, Allstate, Farmers, GEICO, State Farm, Mass Mutual, Northwestern Mutual, New York Life, AFLAC, Liberty Mutual, Prudential
F	AIG, Blue Cross / Blue Shield, Berkshire Hathaway
X	

INSURANCE COMPANIES

WHAT YOU NEED TO KNOW
Whether for our car, health, home, or life, most of us need to buy insurance sooner or later. As we've discovered with the recent corporate bailouts, who we choose to do business with can have serious implications for our collective pocketbooks.

BEST CHOICE
Better World Club

☆ Social Venture Network member
☆ GAM certified Green Business
☆ Only insurance signatory to CERES Principles

WORSE CHOICE
AIG (American International Group)

☠ MM's "Worst Corporation" list for two years[51]
☠ Paid $88 million to Washington lobbyists[12]
☠ $170 billion paid by taxpayers to bailout[54]

WORSE CHOICE
Blue Cross / Blue Shield

☠ #41 in "Top 100 Corporate Criminals"[51]
☠ RS "F" for overall social responsibility[61]
☠ Paid $416 million to Washington lobbyists[12]

JUICE

★	**Organic Valley**
A	Adina, Sambazon, Brew Dr. Kombucha, Tao Kombucha, Equinox, Hex Ferments, Kombucha Botanica
B	Happy Planet, Ginger People, Newman's Own, Santa Cruz Organic, Cascadian Farm, Naked Juice, Florida's Natural, Sunkist
C	Biotta, Horizon, Tree Top, Odwalla, Campbell's, V8, Martinelli's, POM Wonderful, Langer, Hansen's
D	Ocean Spray, Tropicana, Welch's, Jamba Juice, Kern's, RW Knudsen, ReaLemon, Mott's, Snapple, Dole, Del Monte, Sunny Delight
F	Minute Maid, Simply Orange, Hawaiian Punch
X	**Kraft, Back to Nature, Capri Sun, Crystal Light, Kool-Aid, Libby's, Juicy Juice**

JUICE

BUYING TIPS

✓ Purchase organic juices when available
✓ Buy juices in aluminum or glass containers
✓ Avoid plastics whenever possible
✓ Buy larger quantities to reduce packaging

BEST CHOICE

Organic Valley

☆ Small family farmer-owned co-operative
☆ Gives 10% of profits to local community
☆ Humane animal treatment a priority
☆ Ranked #6 best company on the planet

WORST CHOICE

Minute Maid (Coca-Cola)

☠ MM's "Worst Corporation" list for 3 years[51]
☠ Hinders clean water access abroad[22]
☠ Target of major human rights boycotts[30]

WORST CHOICE

Back to Nature (Kraft)

☠ Greenwash Award for public deception[48]
☠ MM's "Worst Corporation" list for five years[51]
☠ Named global climate change laggard[15]
☠ Paid $331 million to Washington lobbyists[12]

LAUNDRY SUPPLIES

★	Seventh Generation, Method, Ecover
A	Earth Friendly, Biokleen, Planet, Earth Breeze, Mountain Green, Mrs. Meyers, CitraSolv, Bio-Pac
B	Lifetree, Country Save, SC Johnson, Bon Ami, Colgate Palmolive, Cold Power, Dynamo, Fab, Spot Shot, Suavitel, Shaklee
C	Static Guard, Fresh Start, Henkel, All, Cuddle Soft, Hurricane, Snuggle, Spree, Sun, Wisk
D	Unilever, Sunlight, Surf, Church & Dwight, Arm & Hammer, Oxi Clean, Xtra, Reckitt Benckiser, Woolite, Calgon, Cling Free, Spray n' Wash, Clorox, Dial, 20 Mule Team Borax, Green Works, Purex
F	Procter & Gamble, Tide, Biz, Bold, Bounce, Cheer, Downy, Drift, Era, Febreze, Gain, Ivory
X	

LAUNDRY SUPPLIES

BUYING TIPS
✓ Avoid plastic containers
✓ Choose refill packages when available
✓ Avoid phosphates and chlorine bleach

BEST CHOICE

Ecover

☆ GAM certified Green Business
☆ Winner, environmental leader award
☆ UN Global 500 Environment Honor Roll
☆ Named 1st sustainable factory in the world

WORST CHOICE

Tide (Procter & Gamble)

☠ Continues unnecessary animal testing[10]
☠ MM's "Worst Corporation" list for two years[51]
☠ GAM "Bottom Rung," responsibility rating[40]
☠ NRDC named "environmental laggard"[53]
☠ Paid $83 million to Washington lobbyists[12]

USEFUL RESOURCES
▱ www.greenamerica.org/livinggreen
▱ www.epa.gov/epp/pubs/cleaning.htm
▱ www.ewg.org/guides/cleaners
▱ www.ecocycle.org

MEAT ALTERNATIVES

⭐	
A	Amy's Kitchen, Turtle Island, Tofurky, Wildwood, Fantastic Foods, Sunshine Burgers, Small Planet, Yves
B	Beyond Meat, Impossible Foods, Field Roast, Nasoya, SoyBoy, Tofu Shop, No Evil
C	Ian's, White Wave, Mori-Nu, Quorn, Alpha, Meatless Farm, Daring, Upton's Naturals
D	Morningstar, Gardenburger
F	Conagra, Gardein, Lightlife
X	Nestlé, Sweet Earth, Kraft, Boca

MEAT ALTERNATIVES

WHAT YOU NEED TO KNOW
Meat alternatives have come a long way since the days of tofu jokes. Burgers, hot dogs, chicken strips, lunch meat, and more are now convincingly tasty in vegetarian form and tend to have a smaller ecological footprint than their counterparts.

BETTER CHOICE
Tofurky (Turtle Island)

☆ EPA Certified 100% Green Power
☆ Highest standards of organic integrity
☆ 1st food sponsor of the Humane Society

WORST CHOICE
Boca Burgers (Kraft)

☠ Greenwash Award for public deception[48]
☠ MM's "Worst Corporation" list for five years[51]
☠ Named global climate change laggard[15]
☠ Paid $331 million to Washington lobbyists[12]

USEFUL RESOURCES
🖥 www.cornucopia.org/soysurvey
🖥 www.organicconsumers.org

MEAT PRODUCTS

✪	**Organic Valley, Organic Prairie, Mighty**
A	Butcher Box, Happy Valley, Walden Local, Headwater Food Hub
B	
C	Underwood, Foster Farms, Empire Kosher, Hickory Farms
D	Perdue, Coleman, Niman Ranch, Pilgrim's Pride, Hormel, Applegate, Dinty Moore, Farmer John, Jennie-O, SPAM, Stagg, Valley Fresh
F	Butterball, Banquet, Healthy Choice, Hebrew National, Slim Jim, Tyson, Ball Park Franks, Jimmy Dean, Hillshire Farms, Smithfield, Conagra, Armour, Cook's, Eckrich, Farmland, Premium Standard, Saag's
X	Kraft, Louis Rich, Oscar Meyer, Libby's

MEAT PRODUCTS

WHAT YOU NEED TO KNOW
Meat production tends to consume more resources than agriculture, so it's especially important to choose sustainable humane options.

BUYING TIPS
✓ Choose free-range, organic meat options

BEST CHOICE

Organic Prairie (Organic Valley)

☆ Small family-farmer cooperative
☆ Gives 10% of profits to local community
☆ Humane animal treatment a priority

WORSE CHOICE

Ball Park Franks (Tyson)

☠ MM's "Worst Corporation" list for two years[51]
☠ CEP 'F' for overall social responsibility[14]
☠ Guilty of 20+ violations of Clean Air Act[61]
☠ #52 in "Top 100 Corporate Criminals"[51]

USEFUL RESOURCES
🖥 www.humanesociety.org
🖥 www.organicconsumers.org
🖥 www.certifiedhumane.org

MEDICAL

★	
A	Traditional Medicinals
B	Medtronic, Tyco
C	Baxter, Biovail
D	Novo Nordisk, Church & Dwight, Del Labs, AbbVie, AstraZeneca, WR Grace, Reckitt, Teva, Mead Johnson, Bristol Myers Squibb
F	Eli Lilly, Johnson & Johnson, Band-Aid, Benadryl, Neosporin, Rolaids, Tylenol, Visine, Roche, Genentech, Berkshire Hathaway, DaVita, Merck, Schering Plough, GSK, Dr. Scholl's, Sanofi, Allegra, Chattem, Cortizone, Merial, Unisom, Novartis, Bayer, Alka-Seltzer, Proctor & Gamble, Vicks, Day/Nyquil, Metamucil, Pepto-Bismol
X	Abbott, Ensure, Vicodin, Pfizer, Advil, Luden's, Pharmacia, Upjohn, Motrin, Wyeth, Kraft, Halls, Purdue

MEDICAL

WHAT YOU NEED TO KNOW
Pharmaceutical companies are some of the most powerful and least responsible of any on the planet. When you do have a choice of medical products, it is very important that you choose the better companies.

BUYING TIPS
✓ Make sure to look on the back of the box to see what company manufactures an item

BEST CHOICE
Traditional Medicinals

☆ GAM certified Green Business
☆ Powered by 100% renewable energy
☆ Utilizes sustainable harvesting of wild herbs
☆ Organic, fair trade, biodynamic ingredients

WORSE CHOICE
Pfizer

⚑ MM's "Worst Corporation" list for five years[51]
⚑ Named "Environmental Laggard" by CEP[14]
⚑ #17 in "Top 100 Corporate Criminals"[51]
⚑ Paid $221 million to Washington lobbyists[12]
⚑ #64 of PERI 100 Most Toxic Water Polluters[58]

MILK & ALTERNATIVES

★	Organic Valley
A	Nancy's, Eden, Straus Family Creamery, Ripple, VitaCoco, WestSoy, Helios, Stonyfield, Clover
B	Pacific, Blue Diamond, Almond Breeze, Califia, Earth/Smart Balance, Forager, Malk, Milkadamia, Mooala, NotMilk, Nutpods, Oatly, Orgain, Planet Oat, Tempt, ZenSoy, VitaSoy, Danone, Horizon, Silk
C	Kikkoman, Daisy, Hood, Lucerne
D	Yoo-Hoo, Soy/Rice/Almond Dream, 8th Continent, Borden, Land O'Lakes, Knudsen
F	Johnson & Johnson, Lactaid, Dairy Ease, Mayfield, Alta Dena, Berkeley Farms, Garelick, Meadow Gold
X	Kraft, Cool Whip, Nestlé, Carnation

MILK & ALTERNATIVES

WHAT YOU NEED TO KNOW
Now there is a wide range of socially responsible
options for both dairy and non-dairy milk lovers.

BEST CHOICE
Organic Valley

☆ Ranked #3 best company on the planet
☆ Small, family farmer-owned co-operative
☆ Humane animal treatment a priority
☆ Gives 10% of profits to local community
☆ Member of the Social Venture Network

WORST CHOICE
Cool Whip (Kraft)

☠ Greenwash Award for public deception[48]
☠ MM's "Worst Corporation" list for five years[51]
☠ Named global climate change laggard[15]
☠ Paid $331 million to Washington lobbyists[12]
☠ Currently the target of 2 major boycotts[22,55]

RESOURCES
🖥 www.organicconsumers.org
🖥 www.cornucopia.org/dairy_brand_ratings

MOBILE PHONES & SERVICE

✪	Fairphone
A	Credo, Working Assets, HP, Nokia, Apple, iPhone, iOS
B	Dell, Google, Pixel, Android, Alcatel, NEC, Kyocera
C	Cingular, Siemens, Vodafone, Motorola, Energizer, Ericsson, nVidia, Garmin, Boost, BenQ, Haier, Casio, Bosch
D	Sprint, Virgin, Nextel, HTC, Fujitsu, Asus, Viewsonic, Toshiba, Samsung, Sony, T-Mobile, Metro, Huawei, Lenovo, ZTE, Vivo, Philips, Panasonic, LG, Sharp, Acer, Mitsubishi, Blackberry
F	Amazon, Microsoft
X	Verizon, AT&T

MOBILE PHONES & SERVICE

WHAT YOU NEED TO KNOW
Cell phones are part of a billion-dollar industry. Make sure that this significant revenue stream is going toward building a better world rather than tearing it apart.

BUYING TIPS
✓ Remember to recycle your old cell phone(s)
✓ Look for solar chargers to reduce energy use

BETTER CHOICE
Credo Mobile (Working Assets)

☆ Given $60 million to a range of nonprofits
☆ Purchases carbon offsets for energy use
☆ Educates for engaged citizenship

WORST CHOICE
Verizon

☠ Given $295 million to Washington lobbyists[12]
☠ CEP 'F' for overall social responsibility[14]
☠ Discriminated against pregnant employees[48]

USEFUL RESOURCES
🖳 www.greenpeace.org/greenerelectronics
🖳 www.opensecrets.org

OFFICE & SCHOOL SUPPLIES

★	
A	Seeds Green Printing, Xerox, HP
B	Interface, Herman Miller, Ricoh, DHL, Staples, Pitney Bowes, Canon
C	BIC, Parker, Schaeffer, Hallmark, USPS, Brother, Epson, Ikon, Zebra, Pilot, Uniball, Henkel, Duck, Airborne Express
D	OfficeMax, Rubbermaid, Sharpie, Expo, Elmer's, Paper Mate, IBM, Smurfit, Avery Dennison, Olympus, UPS, Fedex, 3M, Scotch, Post-It, BASF, Mead, At-A-Glance, Day Runner, Trapper Keeper, Cambridge, Columbian, Five Star
F	
X	

OFFICE & SCHOOL SUPPLIES

WHAT YOU NEED TO KNOW

Many of the items we use during the day are in some way related to our workplace. If you have any potential influence over office purchasing, consider suggesting a shift in funds over to more socially responsible products.

BEST CHOICE

Seeds Green Printing

☆ GAM & B Lab Certified Responsible Business
☆ Environmental leader in the printing industry
☆ 2x named "Best for the World" by B Lab

WORSE CHOICE

Mead (MeadWestvaco)

☻ Named global climate change laggard[19]
☻ Refuses disclosure to consumers[14]
☻ Continues unnecessary animal testing[10]
☻ CEP 'F' for overall social responsibility[14]

USEFUL RESOURCES

⌨ checkyourpaper.panda.org
⌨ www.fsc.org

OIL, VINEGAR, OLIVES, & PICKLES

☆	AlterEco, Canaan Fair Trade, Nutiva
A	Eden, Annie's, Rapunzel, Hain, Spectrum
B	NOW, Ginger People, Bragg, Smart Balance, Cascadian Farm, Newman's Own, Natural Value
C	B&G, Republic of Tea, Armstrong, Canola Harvest, Lindsay, Mezzetta, Mt. Olive, Nakano, Saffola, Star
D	Crisco, Del Monte, Unilever, Heinz
F	Conagra, Wesson, PAM, Bertolli, Vlasic
X	Kraft, Claussen

OIL, VINEGAR, OLIVES, & PICKLES

WHAT YOU NEED TO KNOW
A number of socially responsible companies now offer conventional and organic oils and vinegars.

BUYING TIPS
✓ Choose organic oil, vinegar, & cooking spray

BEST CHOICE
Canaan Fair Trade

☆ GAM certified Green Business
☆ Produces the only fair trade certified olives
☆ Supports Palestinian farmers & communities

WORST CHOICE
Claussen (Kraft)

☠ Greenwash Award for public deception[48]
☠ MM's "Worst Corporation" list for five years[51]
☠ Named global climate change laggard[15]
☠ Paid $331 million to Washington lobbyists[12]

USEFUL RESOURCES
🖳 www.greenpages.org

ONLINE

★	
A	Etsy, Better World Books, Mozilla, Firefox, Wikipedia, Apple, Safari
B	Google, Chrome, YouTube, SquareSpace, Orbitz, Groupon
C	Hulu, eBay, Expedia, Priceline, Kayak, Snapchat, Wordpress, Opera, Zoom, McAfee, ByteDance, TikTok
D	Netflix, Pinterest, Reddit, Twitter, Cox, Flickr, DoubleClick, Charter, Yelp, CenturyLink, Qwest, AOL
F	Facebook, Messenger, WhatsApp, Instagram, Oracle, Peoplesoft, Time Warner, Amazon, IMDb, Microsoft, MSN, Live, Internet Explorer, Bing, LinkedIn, Skype, Comcast
X	Verizon, Xfinity, Yahoo!, AT&T

ONLINE

WHAT YOU NEED TO KNOW
In the information age, what ISP and browser you use is just as important as where you browse. Whenever possible, support those companies and organizations that turn some of your dollars (and clicks) into making a difference on and offline.

BUYING TIPS
✓ Buy local, used items online when possible
✓ Support open source and community efforts

BEST CHOICE

Etsy

☆ B Lab Certified Responsible Company
☆ Major web hub for handmade goods
☆ Supports thousands of small businesses

WORSE CHOICE

Comcast

☠ CEP & RS "F" for overall social responsibility[61]
☠ Paid $234 million to Washington lobbyists[12]
☠ Gave $59 million in campaign contributions[12]
☠ Refuses disclosure to consumers[14]

OUTDOOR GEAR

✪	**Patagonia, Klean Kanteen**
A	REI, Timberland, MiiR, Soma, S'well
B	prAna, Kelty, Sierra Designs, Mountain Equipment Co-op, Chaco, North Face
C	Marmot, Coleman, Eddie Bauer, Garmin, TomTom, Nalgene, Camelback, Osprey, Cotopaxi, Black Diamond, Helly Hansen, Hydro Flask, Arc'teryx, Keen, L.L. Bean, Fjallraven
D	Merrell, Columbia, LuluLemon, Dick's, VF, Jansport, Eastpack, Eagle Creek, Reef
F	Target, Amazon
X	T.J. Maxx, Sierra Trading Post, Walmart

OUTDOOR GEAR

WHAT YOU NEED TO KNOW
While enjoying the outdoors, make certain that the equipment you use is preserving the natural environment rather than helping to destroy it.

BEST CHOICE

Patagonia

☆ Environmental leader in industry
☆ Plastic bottles recycling pioneer — fleece
☆ 1% of sales goes to enviro groups
☆ Powered by 100% renewable energy

BEST CHOICE

Klean Kanteen

☆ B Lab Certified Responsible Company
☆ GAM certified Green Business
☆ 1% of sales goes to enviro groups

WORST CHOICE

Walmart

☠ #3 worst company on the planet[7]
☠ CEP 'F' for overall social responsibility[14]
☠ Sex-discrimination class action lawsuit[48]
☠ Documented exploitation of child labor[61]
☠ Paid $104 million to Washington lobbyists[12]
☠ RS rated worst responsibility in industry[61]

PAPER & PAPER PRODUCTS

★	New Leaf, Seventh Generation
A	Greenline, Earth Friendly, Green Forest, Xerox, HP
B	Mohawk, Cascades, Marcal, Tork, Staples, Kimberly-Clark, Cottonelle, Kleenex, Purely Cotton, Scott, Scotties, Natural Value, Canon
C	Earth Friendly, Brother, Epson, SCA, Wausau, WB Mason
D	OfficeMax, Avery Dennison, 3M, Post-It, FedEx, Weyerhaeuser, Boise, Domtar
F	Hammermill, International Paper, Mead, Cambridge, Procter & Gamble, Bounty, Charmin, Puffs
X	Koch, Georgia Pacific, Angel Soft, Brawny, Dixie, Envision, Mardi Gras, Quilted Northern, Soft n' Gentle, Sparkle, Vanity Fair, Zee

PAPER & PAPER PRODUCTS

WHAT YOU NEED TO KNOW
Just remember one thing: PAPER = TREES.

BUYING TIPS
✓ Look for post-consumer recycled content
✓ Choose non-chlorine bleached paper options

BEST CHOICE

New Leaf

☆ Forest Stewardship Council certified
☆ Offers 100% post-consumer options
☆ Invented the Eco-Audit for books, etc.
☆ Uses sustainably harvested wood

WORST CHOICE

Georgia-Pacific (Koch)

☠ #44 in "Top 100 Corporate Criminals"[51]
☠ GP gives lowest environmental ranking[44]
☠ #8 of PERI 100 Most Toxic Air Polluters[58]
☠ Paid $166 million to Washington lobbyists[12]
☠ EC responsibility rating of VERY POOR[30]

USEFUL RESOURCES
🖥 checkyourpaper.panda.org
🖥 www.fsc.org

PASTA & SAUCE

★	
A	Eden, Amy's Kitchen, Annie's, Simply Organic, Lundberg, Bionaturae, Hain, Deboles, Walnut Acres, Muir Glen
B	Newman's Own, Natural Value
C	General Mills, Betty Crocker, Seeds of Change, Campbell's, Prego, Progresso, Quaker, Golden Grain, Pasta Roni, Barilla, DaVinci, De Cecco, Emeril's, Goya, Halbrand, Manischewitz, Mezzetta, Prince, Ronzoni, Stella
D	Ragu, McCormick, Lawry's, Del Monte, Contadina, Classico, Unilever, Knorr
F	Conagra, Chef Boyardee, Bertolli, Hunt's
X	Kraft, Buitoni, Back to Nature

PASTA & SAUCE

BUYING TIPS
✓ Look for items made with organic ingredients
✓ Buy larger quantities to reduce packaging

BEST CHOICE
Eden Foods

☆ Ranked #28 best company on the planet
☆ CEP's highest social responsibility score
☆ GAM certified Green Business

BEST CHOICE
Amy's Kitchen

☆ Donates food to relief efforts
☆ Produces all-vegetarian, organic foods
☆ GAM certified Green Business

WORST CHOICE
Back To Nature (Kraft)

☠ #4 contributor to Washington lobbyists[12]
☠ Currently the target of two major boycotts[22,55]
☠ Greenwash Award for public deception[48]
☠ Part of #2 worst company on the Earth[7]

USEFUL RESOURCES
🖥 www.greenpages.org
🖥 www.organicconsumers.org

PEANUT BUTTER & JELLY

★	
A	Rapunzel, Bionaturae, Hain, Arrowhead Mills, Maranatha, Robertson's
B	Smart/Earth Balance, Woodstock Farms, Cascadian Farm
C	Justin's, Santa Cruz Organic, Seeds of Change, Bonne Maman, Glick's, Joyva, Manischewitz, Sorrell Ridge, Teddie
D	Welch's, Smucker's, Adams, Goober, Knott's, Laura Scudder's, Simply Fruit, Unilever, Skippy
F	Nutella, Procter & Gamble, Jif, Conagra, Peter Pan
X	Kraft

PEANUT BUTTER & JELLY

BUYING TIPS
✓ Look for items made with organic ingredients
✓ Seek out local farmers markets

BEST CHOICE
Rapunzel

☆ Fair trade & organic leader in food ind.
☆ Supports global sustainable farming
☆ Produced 1st 100% organic chocolate

WORSE CHOICE
Skippy (Unilever)

☠ Continues unnecessary animal testing[10]
☠ EC responsibility rating of VERY POOR[30]
☠ Illegal toxic waste dumping abroad[48]
☠ RS 'D-' for overall social responsibility[61]

WORST CHOICE
Kraft

☠ Named "Top 10 Greenwasher"[48]
☠ Involved in document deletion cover-up[48]
☠ MM's "Worst Corporation" list for five years[51]
☠ Paid $331 million to Washington lobbyists[12]

PET CARE

★	
A	OnlyNaturalPet, PLAY, BioBag, Wildcatch, Swheat Scoop
B	Honest Kitchen, Halo, Dr. Harvey's, PetGuard, Artemis, Natural Balance, V-Dog, Newman's Own, Petco, Karma
C	Breeder's Choice, Avoderm, Canidae, Wellness, Old Mother Hubbard, PetSmart, Holistic Select, Eagle Pack, PHD, VIAND
D	Arm & Hammer, Feline Pine, Del Monte, 9 Lives, Kibbles n' Bits, Meow Mix, Milk Bone, Hill's Science Diet, Blue Buffalo, Heartland, Clorox, Scoop Away
F	Schering Plough, Fresh Step, Mars, Nutro, Pedigree, Royal Canin, Sheba, Sensible Choice, Whiskas, Frontline, Heartgard, Merial, Procter & Gamble, Eukanuba, IAMS
X	Bayer, Advantage/Advantix, Nestlé, Purina, Alpo, Castor & Pollux, Dog Chow, Fancy Feast, Friskies, Gourmet, Merrick, ONE, Tender Vittles, Tidy Cats, Zuke's, Pfizer, Revolution

PET CARE

WHAT YOU NEED TO KNOW
Recent innovations have been made in the area of
socially responsible pet care, so you should have a
number of excellent options to choose from.

BUYING TIPS
✓ Buy pet food made with organic ingredients
✓ Buy cat litter made from renewable sources

BEST CHOICE
BioBag

☆ 100% biodegradable, corn-based material
☆ 100% compostable w/multiple certifications
☆ GAM certified Green Business

WORST CHOICE
Purina (Nestlé)

☠ "Most Irresponsible" corporation award[6]
☠ Involved in child slavery lawsuit[61]
☠ Aggressive takeovers of family farms[61]

USEFUL RESOURCES
🖥 www.greenpages.org
🖥 www.bcorporation.net
🖥 www.responsibleshopper.org

POPCORN, NUTS, PRETZELS, & MIXES

✪	Equal Exchange
A	Eden, Hain, Arrowhead Mills, Bearitos, Little Bear
B	Lesser Evil, Newman's Own, Blue Diamond, NOW
C	General Mills, Chex Mix, Food Should Taste Good, Gardetto's, True North, Robert's American Gourmet, Pirate's Booty, Snyder's
D	United Natural Foods, ExpresSnaks, Diamond, Emerald, Pop Secret, Smucker's, Sahale, Cracker Jack, RoldGold, Smartfood
F	Conagra, Act II, Crunch n' Munch, David, Fiddle Faddle, Orville Redenbacher, Jiffy Pop, Poppycock
X	Kraft, Back to Nature, Corn Nuts, Planters

POPCORN, NUTS, PRETZELS, & MIXES

WHAT YOU NEED TO KNOW
When you're settling in to watch TV or a movie, what you put in that bowl next to the couch makes a big difference for the planet.

BEST CHOICE
Equal Exchange

☆ GAM certified Green Business
☆ Business Ethics Award winner
☆ Industry leader in fair trade movement

BEST CHOICE
Eden Foods

☆ Ranked #28 best company on the planet
☆ CEP's highest social responsibility score
☆ GAM certified Green Business

WORST CHOICE
Planters (Kraft)

☠ Part of #2 worst company on the Earth[7]
☠ Currently the target of 2 major boycotts[22,55]
☠ #4 contributor to Washington lobbyists[12]

USEFUL RESOURCES
🖥 www.responsibleshopper.org

RETAIL STORES

✪	Patagonia
A	Eileen Fisher, REI, Athleta, Timberland, Levi's
B	GAP, Banana Republic, Old Navy, Marks & Spencer, H&M, Reebok, Adidas, Nike, North Face, Ace Hardware
C	IKEA, Eddie Bauer, Best Buy, Burlington Coat Factory, L.L. Bean, Talbot's
D	Dollar General, Dick's Sporting Goods, Bed Bath & Beyond, BJ's Wholesale Club, Ross, Home Depot, Lowe's, JCPenney, Long's Drugs, Rite Aid, Big Lots, Sears, Kmart, Orchard Supply
F	CVS, T.J. Maxx, Target, Walgreens, Costco, Macy's, Disney, Amazon
X	Walmart, Sam's Club

RETAIL STORES

BEST CHOICE

Patagonia

☆ Environmental leader in industry
☆ Plastic bottles recycling pioneer — fleece
☆ 1% of sales goes to enviro groups
☆ Powered by 100% renewable energy

BETTER CHOICE

Timberland

☆ Business Ethics Award winner
☆ 4x Named World's Most Ethical Company
☆ Labelling leader, eco-social footprint
☆ EPA Green Power Award winner

WORST CHOICE

Walmart

☠ #3 worst company on the planet[7]
☠ CEP 'F' for overall social responsibility[14]
☠ Sex-discrimination class action lawsuit[48]
☠ Documented exploitation of child labor[61]
☠ Paid $104 million to Washington lobbyists[12]
☠ RS rated worst responsibility in industry[61]

USEFUL RESOURCES
🖥 www.opensecrets.org
🖥 www.responsibleshopper.org

RICE & OTHER GRAINS

★	Alter Eco
A	Eden, Lotus Foods, Canaan Fair Trade, Bob's Red Mill, Fantastic Foods, Casbah, Lundberg
B	
C	Hodgson Mill, Betty Crocker, Annie Chun's, Carolina Rice, Mahatma, Manischewitz, GOYA, Mrs. Cubbison's, Minute Rice, Quaker, Rice-A-Roni, Seeds of Change, Success Rice
D	Near East, Hungry Jack, Lipton, S&W, Knorr, McCormick, Hormel
F	Uncle Ben's
X	Kraft

RICE & OTHER GRAINS

BUYING TIPS
✓ Look for organic grains
✓ Buy in bulk to reduce packaging waste

BEST CHOICE

Alter Eco

☆ Produces a range of 100% fair trade goods
☆ Works directly with local farmer cooperatives
☆ GAM certified Green Business
☆ Fair trade consumer education leader

BETTER CHOICE

Canaan Fair Trade

☆ GAM certified Green Business
☆ Leader in fair trade integrity standards
☆ Supports Palestinian farmers & communities

WORST CHOICE

Ben's Original (Mars)

☠ CEP 'F' for overall social responsibility[14]
☠ On MM's "10 Worst Corporations" list[51]
☠ Evidence of involvement in child slave labor[61]
☠ Target of international fair trade campaign[25]
☠ "Bottom Rung," Ladder of Responsibility[40]

SALSA, SPREADS, & DIPS

⭐	
A	Simply Organic, Amy's Kitchen , Emerald Valley, Wildwood, Fantastic Foods, Hain, Bearitos, Casbah, Walnut Acres, Native Forest, Muir Glen
B	Newman's Own
C	Old El Paso, Pace, Seeds of Change, Sabra, Nonna Lena, Green Mountain Gringo, Micaela's, Cedar's, Litehouse, Ortega, Haig's, Native, Mrs. Renfro's, Margaritaville
D	Laura Scudder's, Frito-Lay, Tostitos, Lipton, Hormel, Chi Chi's, La Victoria
F	Conagra, Frontera, Rosarita, Salpica
X	Kraft, Taco Bell

SALSA, SPREADS, & DIPS

WHAT YOU NEED TO KNOW
This category includes everything from hummus to salsa to bean dip, and there are responsible choices to be had for every one.

BETTER CHOICE
Amy's Kitchen

☆ Donates food to relief efforts
☆ Produces all-vegetarian organic foods
☆ GAM certified Green Business

BETTER CHOICE
Emerald Valley

☆ Socially Responsible Business Award
☆ 1% to humanitarian & ecological causes
☆ Green Business of the Year Award

WORST CHOICE
Taco Bell (Kraft)

☠ Named "Top 10 Greenwasher"[48]
☠ Involved in document deletion cover-up[48]
☠ MM's "Worst Corporation" list for five years[51]
☠ Paid $331 million to Washington lobbyists[12]

SEAFOOD

⭐	
A	Henry & Lisa's, Whole Foods*, Vital Choice, EcoFish, Wildcatch, Wild Pacific, Blue Horizon Organic, RainCoast
B	HyVee*, Wegmans*, Target*, Safeway*, Aldi*, Vons*, Pak N Save*, Giant Eagle*
C	Ahold*, Delhaize*, Giant*, Stop & Shop*, Peapod*, Albertson's*, Sprouts*, Chicken of the Sea, Crown Prince, Gorton's, Trader Joe's*, Food Lion*, Meijer*, Harris Teeter*
D	Walmart*, Sam's Club*, Neighborhood Market*, Pathmark*, No Frills*, Shop Rite*, Hannaford*, Shop N Save*, Kroger*, Food 4 Less*, Fred Meyer*, King Soopers*, Loaf n Jug*, Quik Stop*, Ralph's*, Kwik Shop*, Bumble Bee, Southeastern Grocers*, Star*, Costco*, Albertsons*, Lucky*, Save A Lot*, Shaws*, Cub Foods*, Bigg's*, Jewel-Osco*
F	Bi-Lo*, Roundy's*, Win-Dixie*, HEB*, WinCo*, A&P*
X	Wakefern*, Price Chopper*, Save Mart*, Publix*

SEAFOOD

WHAT YOU NEED TO KNOW
One of the most important changes you can make
is in choosing ecologically responsible seafood.
While seafood brands are rated in the usual way in
the chart on the left, supermarkets are also rated
here solely based on the sustainability of their seafood selection and are noted with an asterisk (*).

BUYING TIPS
✓ Look for sustainable fishing labels
✓ Local freshwater is often a good choice
✓ See next section for more seafood guidance

BEST CHOICE
Henry & Lisa's

☆ Only environmentally sustainable fishing
☆ Conservation scientists advisory board
☆ Result of marine conservation groups

BETTER CHOICE
Wildcatch

☆ Certified by Marine Stewardship Council
☆ Harvests only sustainable, wild seafood
☆ Works with nonprofits like Salmon Nation

SHOES

☆	Patagonia
A	Dansko, Allbirds, Simple Shoes, Therafit, Sole Rebels, VEJA, Newton Running, The Root Collective, Oliberte, Nisolo, Paez, REI, TOMS, Timberland
B	Birkenstock, Hoka, Sanuk, Teva, UGG, Chaco, Red Wing, Reebok, DMX, Rockport, Adidas, Nike, North Face, Puma, Zappos
C	Ecco, Salomon, Dunlop, Everlast, Hush Puppies, Umbro, Ellesse, HI-TEC, Crocs, Keen, DC, Champion, Eddie Bauer, L.L. Bean, K-Swiss, Lotto
D	Stride Rite, Keds, Sperry, Pentland, Tommy Hilfiger, Converse, Florsheim, Nunn Bush, Saucony, ASICS, Mizuno, DSW, Vans, Foot Locker, Merrell, Brooks, LA Gear, Reef, FILA, Converse, Skechers, Land's End
F	Amazon, DEPARTMENT STORE BRANDS
X	Walmart

WHAT YOU NEED TO KNOW

Almost all store-bought shoes are made in factories in the developing world. The real questions are: How are the workers treated? Are they safe? And do they make enough of a wage to live decently? Your choices here will determine the answers to those questions for tens of thousands of families.

BETTER CHOICE

Dansko

☆ GAM certified Green Business
☆ Powered by 100% renewable energy
☆ LEED Gold eco-certified main office

WORSE CHOICE

LA Gear

☠ Named "Sweatshop Laggard"[14]
☠ CEP 'F' for overall social responsibility[14]
☠ Weak supplier code of conduct for workers[14]

USEFUL RESOURCES

🖥 www.cleanclothes.org
🖥 en.maquilasolidarity.org
🖥 www.free2work.org
🖥 www.labourbehindthelabel.org

SOAP

★	**Dr. Bronner's, Method, EO**
A	Pangea Organics, Canaan Fair Trade, Aubrey, Juniper Ridge, Kiss My Face, Tom's of Maine, Jason, Alba, Oregon Soap Co.
B	Lush, Body Shop, Sappo Hill, Colgate, Irish Spring, Palmolive, Softsoap, Hugo, Zum Bar, Shikai, Clearly Natural
C	Avalon Organics, Burt's Bees, Nature's Gate, Germ-X, Nivea, Coastal
D	Curel, Unilever, Axe, Bioré, Caress, Dove, Jergen's, Lever 2000, St. Ives, Suave, Vaseline, Dial, Tone, Pure & Natural, Coast
F	Johnson & Johnson, Aveeno, Purell, Proctor & Gamble, Gillette, Ivory, Lava, Olay, Old Spice, Safeguard, Zest
X	

SOAP

BUYING TIPS
✓ Choose soaps that aren't tested on animals
✓ Buy USDA Certified Biobased soaps

BEST CHOICE

Dr. Bronner's

☆ Leader in organic standards integrity
☆ 5:1 CEO-to-worker salary cap
☆ Profits donated to variety of causes
☆ Liquid soaps in 100% recycled plastic
☆ Does not test on animals

BETTER CHOICE

Pangea Organics

☆ GAM certified Green Business
☆ Never tests ingredients on animals
☆ 2x Award Winner for Business Ethics

WORST CHOICE

Ivory (Procter & Gamble)

☠ MM's "Worst Corporation" list for two years[51]
☠ Continues unnecessary animal testing[10]
☠ "Bottom Rung," Ladder of Responsibility[40]
☠ Spent over $83 million on lobbyists[12]

SODA

★	**Guayaki**
A	Maine Root, Brew Dr., DASH, Equinox, Hex Ferments, Kombucha Botanica, Sambazon, Tao, Torani, Zevia, Oogave, Sipp
B	Steaz, Ginger People, Newman's Own, Santa Cruz Organic, Spindrift, Reed's
C	Jolt, Shasta, Hansen, Blue Sky, Martinelli's, Hi-Ball, Thomas Kemper, Boylan
D	Soda Stream, Jones, Clearly Canadian, Crystal Geyser, Polar, AriZona, Snapple, 7Up, A&W, Canada Dry, Crush, Dr Pepper, Hires, IBC, Orangina, RC Cola, Squirt, Stewart's, Sunkist, Welch's, Pepsi, Izze, Mountain Dew, Mug, Sierra Mist, Slice, Henry Weinhard's
F	Coca-Cola, Barq's, Fanta, Fresca, Minute Maid, Moxie, Pibb, Sprite
X	**Nestlé, San Pellegrino**

SODA

WHAT YOU NEED TO KNOW
If you're like most people, soda is a daily part of your diet. Move up on the responsible soda chain to avoid companies that are wrecking the planet.

BUYING TIPS
✓ Buy soda in aluminum or glass containers

BETTER CHOICE
Maine Root

☆ Offers fair trade certified sodas
☆ Organic soda industry leader
☆ Local deliveries made using biodiesel
☆ Supports sustainable farming practices

WORSE CHOICE
Coca-Cola

☠ MM's "Worst Corporation" list for three years[51]
☠ Hinders clean water access abroad[22]
☠ Target of major human rights boycotts[30]

USEFUL RESOURCES
🖳 www.ethicalconsumer.org
🖳 www.multinationalmonitor.org
🖳 www.stopcorporateabuse.org

SOUPS, NOODLES, & CURRIES

⭐	
A	Eden, Amy's, Annie's, Fantastic Foods, Hain, Casbah, Health Valley, Imagine, Westbrae, Walnut Acres, Edward & Sons, Native Forest, Nile Spice, Rapunzel, Muir Glen
B	Ginger People, Pacific Natural, Nasoya
C	General Mills, Progresso, Campbell's, Thai Kitchen, Annie Chun's, Alessi, Bar Harbor, Bear Creek, Dr. Maruchan, McDougall's, Nissin, Snow's, Spice Hunter, Sun Luck, Swanson, Tasty Bite, Seeds of Change
D	Lipton, Cup-a-Soup, Unilever, Knorr, Hormel, Herb Ox
F	Mars, Tasty Bite, Conagra, Healthy Choice, Swanson
X	Kraft, Mrs. Grass

SOUPS, NOODLES, & CURRIES

WHAT YOU NEED TO KNOW
Whether it's instant noodles or pea soup, there are many excellent choices for hot, steaming, socially responsible meals.

BUYING TIPS
✓ Look for soups made with organic ingredients

BEST CHOICE
Eden Foods

☆ Ranked #28 best company on the planet
☆ CEP's highest social responsibility score
☆ GAM certified Green Business

WORSE CHOICE
Healthy Choice (Conagra)

☠ MM's "Worst Corporation" list for two years[51]
☠ #50 in "Top 100 Corporate Criminals"[51]
☠ CERES "Climate Change Laggard"[15]

USEFUL RESOURCES
🖥 www.responsibleshopper.org
🖥 www.multinationalmonitor.org
🖥 www.ceres.org

SUGAR, SPICES, & SWEETENERS

★	Alter Eco
A	Eden, King Arthur, Bob's Red Mill, Wholesome Sweeteners, Spectrum, Ener-G, Hain, Arrowhead Mills, Rapunzel, Lundberg, Coombs
B	NOW, Bragg
C	Mrs. Butterworth's, Butter Buds, C&H, Domino, Florida Crystals, Goya, Morton, Spice Hunter, Spike, Sugar in the Raw, Sweet'N Low
D	McCormick, Adolph's, Lawry's, Schilling, Unilever, Molly McButter, Mrs. Dash, Sugar Twin
F	Johnson & Johnson, Splenda
X	Monsanto, NutraSweet, Equal

SUGAR, SPICES, & SWEETENERS

WHAT YOU NEED TO KNOW
Many of these items we buy once and keep using for years. If you want to make a difference while saving your budget, start here.

BUYING TIPS
✓ Buy in bulk to reduce packaging waste

BETTER CHOICE
Wholesome Sweeteners

☆ 1st US fair trade certified sugar available
☆ Actively supports sustainable farming
☆ Makes a full line of organic sweeteners

WORST CHOICE
NutraSweet (Monsanto)

♟ MM's "Worst Corporation" list for three years[51]
♟ #72 of PERI 100 Most Toxic Air Polluters[58]
♟ Paid $79 million to Washington lobbyists[12]
♟ RS 'D-' for overall social responsibility[61]

USEFUL RESOURCES
🖥 www.free2work.org
🖥 www.organicconsumers.org
🖥 www.responsibleshopper.org

SUPERMARKETS

✪	FOOD CO-OPS, FARMERS MARKETS
A	Whole Foods
B	Hy-Vee, Wegmans, Raley's, Food Lion, Trader Joe's, Fresh & Easy
C	Sprouts, Nugget, Pathmark, Weis, No Frills, Weis, Fry's
D	Full Circle, Giant Eagle, C&S, Harris Teeter, Shop Rite, Hannaford, Shop 'n Save, Bi-Lo, Southeastern, Ahold, Delhaize, Giant, Stop & Shop, Peapod, Martin's, Safeway, Carrs, Vons, Pak N Save, Pavilions, Mrs. Wright's, Bon Appetit, Dominiks, A&P, Roundy's, Price Chopper, WinCo, Wakefern, Meijer, HEB, Save Mart, Winn-Dixie, SuperValu, Albertson's, Lucky, Save A Lot, Shaw's, Star, Cub Foods, Bigg's, Jewel-Osco
F	Target, Kroger, Food 4 Less, Fred Meyer, King Soopers, Loaf 'N Jug, Quik Stop, Ralph's, Foods Co, QFC, Turkey Hill, Kwik Shop, Publix, Costco
X	Walmart

SUPERMARKETS

WHAT YOU NEED TO KNOW
If you have a choice, changing where you shop is an incredibly powerful action that will support people and the planet above profit.

BEST CHOICE
Whole Foods

☆ BE's "Best Corporations" list for three years
☆ HQ Powered by 100% renewable energy
☆ Business Ethics Award winner
☆ Established animal & poverty foundation
☆ Created animal compassion standards
☆ Leader in sourcing sustainable seafood

WORST CHOICE
Walmart

☠ MM's "Worst Corporation" list for three years[51]
☠ Major toxic-waste dumping fines[25]
☠ #3 worst company on the planet[4]
☠ CEP 'F' for overall social responsibility[14]
☠ Documented exploitation of child labor[61]
☠ Paid $104 million to Washington lobbyists[12]

USEFUL RESOURCES
🖳 www.localharvest.org
🖳 www.cooperativegrocer.coop

TEA

✪	**Guayaki, Equal Exchange, Numi**
A	Traditional Medicinals, Eco Teas, Organic India, Tulsi, Choice, Zhena's, Bhakti Chai, Rishi, Arbor, Davidson, Oregon Chai, Sencha Naturals, Bigelow, Celestial Seasonings, Honest Tea
B	Kopali, Mighty Leaf, TAZO, Pacific Natural, Tao of Tea, Newman's Own
C	Republic of Tea, Coffee Bean & Tea Leaf, Starbucks, Harney & Sons, Ito En, Stash, Triple Leaf, Yogi Tea, Twinings, Tejava, Tetley, Good Earth
D	AriZona, Jones, Lipton, Snapple, Unilever, Red Rose
F	Procter & Gamble, PG Tips, Coca-Cola, Gold Peak
X	**Nestlé, Sweet Leaf**

TEA

WHAT YOU NEED TO KNOW
If you drink tea, you have an incredible selection of
human- and planet-friendly varieties to pick from.

BUYING TIPS
✓ Look first for the fair trade label, then move on
  to organic, sustainably harvested, etc.

BEST CHOICE
Equal Exchange

☆ GAM certified Green Business
☆ Business Ethics Award winner
☆ Industry leader in fair trade movement

BEST CHOICE
Numi

☆ GAM certified Green Business
☆ Member of the Social Venture Network
☆ Socially Responsible Business Award

WORST CHOICE
Nestea (Nestlé)

☠ Involved in child slavery lawsuit[61]
☠ Baby formula human rights boycott[48]
☠ Involved in union busting outside US[61]
☠ "Most Irresponsible" corporation award[6]

TOYS & GAMES

✪	
A	Apple, Mac, iOS
B	Google, Android OS, LEGO, Mattel, Fisher-Price, Hot Wheels, Matchbox
C	Crayola, Electronic Arts, Warner Bros, Namco, Sega, Ubisoft, Wham-O
D	GameStop, Blizzard, Activision, Sony, Playstation, Hasbro, Milton Bradley, Nerf, Parker Brothers, Play-Doh, Playskool, Tonka, Wizards of the Coast
F	Disney, Nintendo, Switch, Wii, Microsoft, Xbox, Windows, PC
X	

TOYS & GAMES

WHAT YOU NEED TO KNOW
The irresponsible manufacturing of toys and games does not always directly threaten us or our children, but it always endangers people or the environment in some part of the world.

BUYING TIPS
✓ Look for less common, cooperative games
✓ Buy used toys and games when available
✓ Seek out shareware and open-source games

BETTER CHOICE
Apple

☆ Industry leader in reducing conflict minerals
☆ Member, Fair Labor Association
☆ EPA, 100% Green Power Purchaser

WORSE CHOICE
Xbox (Microsoft)

☠ Named "abusive monopoly" by US Court[48]
☠ Paid $193 million to Washington lobbyists[12]
☠ Greenpeace "Green Electronics Laggard"[44]
☠ Refuses disclosure on its business[14]

USEFUL RESOURCES
🖥 www.greenpeace.org
🖥 www.free2work.org

TRAVEL

★	Patagonia
A	TerraPass, Native Energy, CarbonFund, Couchsurfing Intl, Timberland, ZipCar
B	Google Flights, Orbitz, CarbonNeutral, Kelty, North Face, Disney Cruises
C	Lyft, Hotels.com, Priceline, Kayak, Expedia, Samsonite, ebags, Amtrak, Dollar, Hertz, Enterprise, 3 Degrees, Chicago Climate Exchange, Live Neutral, Standard Carbon, Versus Carbon Neutral, Sea World, Silversea Cruises, Uber
D	Yelp, Eagle Creek, Jansport, Wynn Resorts, Royal Carribbean, Celebrity Cruises, Virgin Voices, Regent Seven Seas, Oceania, Norwegian Cruises
F	Cunard, P&O, Princess Cruises, Holland America, Seaborn, AIDA, MSC, Carnival Cruises, Crystal, Costa
X	

TRAVEL

WHAT YOU NEED TO KNOW
While categories like airlines and hotels are large
enough to be listed separately, this chart includes
everything else you might need on your travels:
luggage, car rentals, cruise lines, travel sites, and
carbon offset services.

BETTER CHOICE

TerraPass

☆ B Lab Certified Responsible Company
☆ GAM certified Green Business
☆ Achieved Greenopia's highest eco-score

WORSE CHOICE

Jansport (Vanity Fair)

☠ "Bottom Rung," Ladder of Responsibility[40]
☠ Refuses disclosure to consumers[14]
☠ EC responsibility rating of VERY POOR[30]
☠ Named global climate change laggard[19]
☠ CEP 'F' for overall social responsibility[14]

USEFUL RESOURCES
🖥 sustainabletravelinternational.org
🖥 www.gstcouncil.org

VITAMINS & SUPPLEMENTS

⭐	
A	Traditional Medicinals, New Chapter, Garden of Life, Country Life, Deva, The Honest Company, Oregon's Wild Harvest
B	NOW, SuperNutrition, Vega
C	Nutribiotic, Earthrise, Viactiv, Nature Made, All One, Solaray, Nature's Way, Wellesse, Kikkoman, Country Life, VegLife, Nature's Plus, Weil, Source Naturals, GNC, Jarrow, Carlson
D	Clorox, Rainbow Light, Renew Life, Reckitt Benckiser, Schiff
F	Sanofi, Nature's Own, Bayer, Flintstones, One A Day, Monsanto, Solgar
X	Abbott, Ensure, Similac, Pfizer, Wyeth, Centrum, Emergen-C, Nestlé, Ester-C, Nature's Bounty, Osteo Bi-Flex, Puritan's Pride, Solgar, Sundown

VITAMINS

BUYING TIPS

✓ Look for organic ingredients in supplements
✓ Buy in recyclable bottles: #1, #2, or glass
✓ Purchase in bulk to reduce packaging waste

BETTER CHOICE

New Chapter

☆ Organic, sustainable harvesting practices
☆ International biodynamic certification
☆ Extensive environmental awards
☆ Promotes efforts to sustain biodiversity

WORSE CHOICE

One A Day (Bayer)

☠ #3 of PERI 100 Most Toxic Air Polluters[58]
☠ #78 of PERI 100 Most Toxic Water Polluters[58]
☠ Paid $132 million to Washington lobbyists[12]
☠ MM's "Worst Corporation" list for two years[51]
☠ BD's "Most Irresponsible" corporation award[6]

WORST CHOICE

Centrum (Pfizer)

☠ #64 of PERI 100 Most Toxic Water Polluters[58]
☠ #17 in "Top 100 Corporate Criminals"[51]
☠ Paid $221 million to Washington lobbyists[12]
☠ MM's "Worst Corporation" list for four years[51]

WATER

★	TAP/FILTERED, Klean Kanteen
A	MiiR, Soma, S'well, Love, Dopper, Ocean, 24Bottles, Healthy Human, LifeStraw, memobottle, WAMI
B	Danone, Evian, Volvic
C	Camelback, Nalgene, VOSS, Adirondack, Ethos, Fiji, Fruit2O, Hawaii, Ice Age, Icelandic Glacial, La Croix, Liquid Death, MetroMint, Penta, Sparkletts, Trinity
D	Soda Stream, AriZona, Crystal Geyser, Polar, Canada Dry, Pepsi, Aquafina, Propel, SoBe, K2O
F	Snapple, Deja Blue, Schweppes, Coca-Cola, Dasani, Glaceau, Vitamin Water, Smart Water
X	Nestlé, Acqua Panna, Arrowhead, Calistoga, Crystal Springs, Deer Park, Essentia, Ice Mountain, Ozarka, Perrier, Poland Spring, Pure Life, San Pellegrino, Vittel, Zephyr Hills

WATER

BUYING TIPS
✓ Carry your own reusable bottle
✓ Buy fewer, larger bottles, and refill them
✓ ALWAYS recycle the bottles when done

BEST CHOICE
Klean Kanteen

☆ B Lab Certified Responsible Company
☆ GAM certified Green Business
☆ 1% of sales goes to enviro groups

WORSE CHOICE
Dasani (Coca-Cola)

☠ MM's "Worst Corporation" list for three years[51]
☠ Hinders clean water access abroad[22]
☠ Target of major human rights boycotts[30]

WORST CHOICE
Arrowhead (Nestlé)

☠ Baby formula human rights boycott[48]
☠ "Most Irresponsible" corporation award[6]
☠ Involved in child slavery lawsuit[61]

USEFUL RESOURCES
🖥 www.thinkoutsidethebottle.org
🖥 www.greenpeace.org

WINE

⭐	LOCAL VINEYARDS
A	Fetzer, Frey, A to Z, Bainbridge, Chateau Maris, Cape Venture, Chehalem, Concha y Toro, David Hill, Lubanzi, Morne, Perlage, Salcheto, Sokol Blosser, Stoller, Symington
B	La Rocca, Frog's Leap, Kunde Estates, Alma Rosa, Banrock Station, Benziger, Bota Box, Cline, French Rabbit, Kendall Jackson, Mountain Meadows, Rodney Strong, Sobon Estate, St. Francis
C	Almaden, Demetria, Estancia, Franzia, Grgich Hills, Inglewood, Jacob's Creek, Lindeman's, Luna di Luna, Paul Masson, Sutter Home, Andrés, Blossom Hill, Bonny Doon, Cakebread, Carlo Rossi, Corbett Canyon, Dom Perignon, Ecco Domani, Gallo, Krug Champagne, Mondavi, Sterling, Turning Leaf
D	Barefoot, Charles Shaw, Duckhorn, Korbel, Rombauer, Silver Oak, Yellow Tail
F	
X	

WINE

BUYING TIPS

✓ Look for organic wine varieties on the shelf
✓ Support local vineyards — try their wine
✓ Buy in bulk to reduce packaging waste

BEST CHOICE

Fetzer

☆ Powered by 100% renewable energy
☆ All vineyards certified organic
☆ Reduced production waste by 94%
☆ Bottles are 40% recycled glass
☆ BE Award for Environmental Excellence

BEST CHOICE

Frey

☆ GAM certified Green Business
☆ Oldest organic US winery
☆ 1st US biodynamic wine producer

BEST CHOICE

A to Z

☆ 1st B Corp Certified US Winery
☆ Supports local sustainable farming practices
☆ B Corp names them "Best for the World" Co.

PRODUCT CATEGORY INDEX

Lip Balm	Body Care
Luggage	Travel
Margarine	Butter & Margarine
Marshmallows	Baked Goods & Baking Supplies
Mayonnaise	Condiments & Dressings
Mouthwash	Dental Care
Mustard	Condiments & Dressings
Noodles	Soup, Noodles, & Curries
Nuts	Popcorn, Nuts, Pretzels, & Mixes
Package Delivery	Office & School Supplies
Pain Relievers	Medical
Pancake Mix	Breakfast Food
Pencils & Pens	Office & School Supplies
Pickles	Oil, Vinegar, Olives, & Pickles
Pies	Desserts
Pizza	Frozen Dinners
Potato Chips	Chips
Pretzels	Popcorn, Nuts, Pretzels, & Mixes
Pudding	Dairy Products
Rice Milk	Milk & Alternatives
Salt	Sugar, Spices, & Sweeteners

School Supplies	Office & School Supplies
Shampoo	Hair Care
Shaving Needs	Body Care
Soft Drinks	Soda
Soy Milk	Milk & Alternatives
Sports Drinks	Energy Drinks
Sun Block	Body Care
Syrup	Sugar, Spices, & Sweeteners
Tahini	Peanut Butter & Jelly
Tampons	Feminine Care
Tape	Office & School Supplies
Tissues	Paper & Paper Products
Tofu	Meat Alternatives
Toilet Paper	Paper & Paper Products
Tomato Paste	Pasta & Sauce
Toothbrushes	Dental Care
Toothpaste	Dental Care
Tuna	Seafood
Veggie Burgers	Meat Alternatives
Vinegar	Oil, Vinegar, Olives, & Pickles
Video Games	Toys & Games
Waffles	Breakfast Food
Whipped Cream	Dairy Products
Yogurt	Dairy Products

DATA SOURCES

1. 1% For The Planet [onepercentfortheplanet.org]
2. American Humane [americanhumane.org]
3. American Sustainable Business Council
   [asbcouncil.org]
4. As You Sow [asyousow.org]
5. B Corporations [bcorporation.net]
6. Berne Declaration [bernedeclaration.ch]
7. Better World Shopper [betterworldshopper.org]
8. Business Ethics [business-ethics.com]
9. Business for Social Responsibility [bsr.org]
10. Caring Consumer [caringconsumer.org]
11. Center for Public Integrity [publicintegrity.org]
12. Center for Responsive Politics [opensecrets.org]
13. Center For Science in the Public Interest
    [cspinet.org]
14. CEP (Council on Economic Priorities) [archive.org]
15. CERES [ceres.org]
16. Clean Clothes Campaign [cleanclothes.org]
17. Clean Computer Campaign [svtc.org]
18. Clean Up Fashion [labourbehindthelabel.org]
19. Climate Counts [climatecounts.org]
20. Consumers Union [consumersunion.org]
21. Cornucopia Institute [cornucopia.org]
22. Corporate Accountability International
    [stopcorporateabuse.org]
23. Corporate Critic [corporatecritic.org]
24. Corporate Knights [corporateknights.com]
25. Corpwatch [corpwatch.org]

DATA SOURCES

26. Covalence EthicalQuote [covalence.ch]

27. CSRwire [csrwire.com]

28. Electronic Industry Citizenship Coalition
      [eiccoalition.org]

29. Electronics TakeBack Coalition
      [electronicstakeback.com]

30. Ethical Consumer [ethicalconsumer.org]

31. Ethical Trading Initiative [ethicaltrade.org]

32. Ethisphere [ethisphere.com]

33. Fair Labor Association [fairlabor.org]

34. Fair Trade Federation [fairtradefederation.org]

35. Fast Company [fastcompany.com]

36. Forest Ethics [forestethics.org]

37. Free2Work [free2work.org]

38. Global Exchange [globalexchange.org]

39. Global Sullivan Principles
      [thesullivanfoundation.org/gsp]

40. Green America [greenamerica.org]

41. Green Cross International [gci.ch]

42. Green-e [green-e.org]

43. Greenopia [greenopia.com]

44. Greenpeace [greenpeace.org]

45. Hoovers [hoovers.com]

46. Human Rights Campaign [hrc.org]

47. International Labor Rights Forum
      [laborrights.org]

48. Know More [archive.org]

DATA SOURCES

49. Labour Behind the Label
    [labourbehindthelabel.org]
50. Maquila Solidarity Network [maquilasolidarity.org]
51. Multinational Monitor [multinationalmonitor.org]
52. National Association for the Advancement of
    Colored People [naacp.org]
53. Natural Resources Defense Council [nrdc.org]
54. The New York Times [newyorktimes.com]
55. Organic Consumers Assn [organicconsumers.org]
56. Oxfam International [oxfam.org]
57. Oceana International [oceana.org]
58. Political Economy Research Institute
    [peri.umass.edu]
59. Rainforest Action Network [ran.org]
60. Responsible Purchasing Network
    [responsiblepurchasing.org]
61. Responsible Shopper [responsibleshopper.org]
62. Responsible Sourcing Network
    [sourcingnetwork.org]
63. Restaurant Opportunities Centers United
    [rocunited.org]
64. Sierra Club [sierraclub.org]
65. Social Accountability International [sai-intl.org]
66. Social Venture Network [svn.org]
67. Socially Responsible Business Awards
    [sociallyresponsibleawards.org]
68. Transfair USA [transfairusa.org]
69. Union of Concerned Scientists [ucsusa.org]

DATA SOURCES

70. U.S. Environmental Protection Agency [epa.gov]
71. U.S. Securities & Exchange Commission [sec.gov]
72. Vegan Action [vegan.org]
73. The Washington Post [washingtonpost.com]
74. WorldBlu [worldblu.com]
75. World Environment Center [wec.org]
76. World Wildlife Fund [worldwildlife.org]

NEW SOURCES

77. Violation Tracker [corp-research.org]
78. Center for Media & Democracy [prwatch.org]
79. Federal Trade Commission [ftc.gov]
80. The Wall Street Journal [wsj.com]
81. U.S. Department of Justice [justice.gov]

About the Author

Since receiving his doctoral degree in sociology at the University of Colorado, Boulder, Ellis Jones has focused all of his energies on bridging the gap between academics, activists, and the average citizen. A scholar of social responsibility, global citizenship, and everyday activism, Dr. Jones continues to teach and give presentations across the country on how to turn lofty ideals into practical actions. His other work includes The Better World Handbook (winner of Spirituality & Health's Best Book of the Year Award for 2002 under the category of Hope).

Dr. Jones has given inspiring yet practical presentations to a wide variety of audiences, including colleges and universities, businesses, churches, sustainability symposiums, service conferences, and global citizenship summits.

He has been interviewed for radio and television in both the US and Canada and was featured in the documentary film *50 Ways To Save The Planet*. In 2005, his work inspired the creation of The Better World Handbook Festival in Vancouver, BC. In 2021, a short documentary focused on his work premiered at the CO Environmental Film Festival, *Every Dollar Is A Vote*.

Ellis Jones has lived, studied, and worked in many parts of Europe, Asia, and Central America. He has won numerous awards for his work in the classroom and has taught at CU Boulder, UC Davis, Sac City College and is currently an Associate Professor of Sociology at College of the Holy Cross in Worcester, MA.

If you are interested in learning more about how you can support this work or would like to schedule a speaking engagement, please send an email to:

sodoctorjones@gmail.com

NOTES